Drive and Stroll in

Suffolk

———————•———————

Cyril Francis

COUNTRYSIDE BOOKS
NEWBURY BERKSHIRE

Photographs by the author
Maps by Gelder Design & Mapping

Cover picture of Kersey
supplied by Jonathan Steed

Designed by Peter Davies, Nautilus Design

Produced through MRM Associates Ltd., Reading
Typeset by CJWT Solutions, St Helens
Printed by Cambridge University Press

Contents

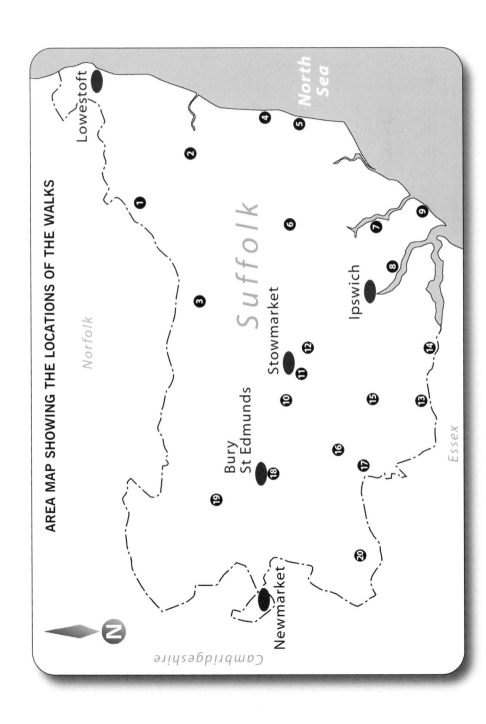

AREA MAP SHOWING THE LOCATIONS OF THE WALKS

Contents ✍

PUBLISHER'S NOTE

We hope that you obtain considerable enjoyment from this book; great care has been taken in its preparation. Although at the time of publication all routes followed public rights of way or permitted paths, diversion orders can be made and permissions withdrawn.

We cannot, of course, be held responsible for such diversion orders and any inaccuracies in the text which result from these or any other changes to the routes nor any damage which might result from walkers trespassing on private property. We are anxious though that all details covering the walks are kept up to date and would therefore welcome information from readers which would be relevant to future editions.

The simple sketch maps that accompany the walks in this book are based on notes made by the author whilst checking out the routes on the ground. However, for the benefit of a proper map, we do recommend that you purchase the relevant Ordnance Survey sheet covering your walk. The Ordnance Survey maps are widely available, especially through booksellers and local newsagents.

Introduction ♘

As the name suggests, this book is all about driving to an attractive spot, taking a leisurely stroll, followed perhaps by a hearty meal at a local pub or café. Inside the covers you'll find a varied selection of routes, including, hopefully, some new ones plus one or two old favourites. The walks are aimed not so much at seasoned ramblers who prefer longer distances but more at casual walkers who want to stroll at their own pace, stopping at places of interest and savouring the local atmosphere.

Depending on the route taken you will walk on a variety of terrains. The most gentle route takes you along a dismantled stretch of an historic railway, or you will explore river foreshores and field edge paths, forest glades, and muddy creeks, cliff tops and shingle beaches – breathing in the bracing sea air. In Suffolk you really are spoilt for choice.

Items and places of interest waiting to be discovered en route include the remains of an old minster and a Benedictine abbey, complete with its prize-winning gardens, a remarkable doom-painting, a stretch of the country's longest crinkle-crankle wall, a magnificent moated Tudor hall and countryside immortalized by the famous landscape painter, John Constable. In addition, there are three grand churches to admire and a cathedral which has finally been completed with the building of a Gothic tower. Of course, nothing ever stays the same in the countryside. As you go, remember to take a look at the broader picture – the people, the villages, the farming, all the things that affect the Suffolk landscape.

Though most of the walks feature a pub – a welcome stop for a refreshing pint on a summer's day, or a cosy fire on a crisp winter's morning – I've also mentioned food and drink available at cafés and country parks. Alternatively you could take a picnic with you. Several locations have outside facilities including tables and toilets.

The book includes detailed route-finding directions but always take a good map – preferably the Ordnance Survey Explorer series. The map also comes in handy if wish to extend a walk, possibly linking up with other paths. Perhaps you will be selective, or walk all the routes mentioned. Whatever you decide, I hope you enjoy walking in this county as I have done. Experience its rich variety of texture, mood, colour and tranquillity while you can.

So, what are you waiting for? You've bought the book, now select a walk and start the car. It's time to go.

Cyril Francis

1 | St Cross South Elmham

Milking time at South Elmham

The Walk 2½ miles ⏱ 1½ hours
Map OS Explorer No 231 Southwold & Bungay (GR 308834)

How to get there

The small village of St Cross South Elmham lies some 5 miles south-west of Bungay. From the Ipswich or Norwich directions take the A140 and then join the A143 at Scole. After the Harleston bypass turn right onto the B1062 signposted to Flixton and Homersfield. Look for brown signs directing you along a minor road (about 2 miles) to South Elmham Hall. **Parking**: Ample parking at South Elmham Hall.

Drive and Stroll

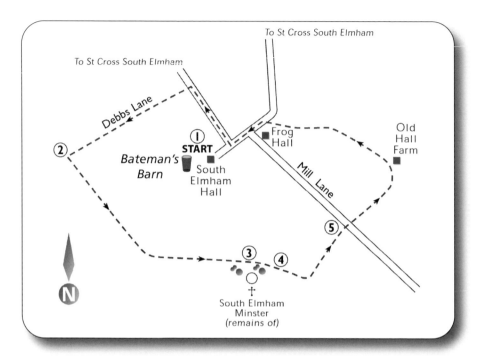

Introduction

This short stroll takes place in an overlooked area in north Suffolk collectively known as Saints Country. The map shows a host of small villages with names such as St Margaret, St James, St Michael, St Cross and All Saints. The stroll begins at South Elmham Hall, a 16th-century moated manor house and originally an old hunting lodge dating from around 1275. Stories of mystery and legend surround the site with echoes of an ancient landscape.

The present owner has introduced a number of permissive paths, augmenting public rights of way, thus enabling walkers to enjoy rural countryside that includes a former deer park and the ruins of an old minster. The distance of the featured walk is an easy 2½ miles. There are other different routes of varying length, details of which are contained in a wildlife walks leaflet obtainable from Bateman's Barn.

Bateman's Barn

Sited in former stables close to the South Elmham Hall farmhouse, a 16th-century barn incorporating flint walls from earlier medieval buildings has been converted into a spacious café and dining area. Bacon and egg breakfasts are served until midday. Other meals on the menu include the likes of pasta and beef risotto. There's also a selection of home-made cakes, plus tea and coffee. Walkers can use the barn's toilets, but are requested to take muddy footwear off before entering the barn. As opening times vary, it's advisable to phone for details in advance. Telephone: 01986 782526. When they are closed, a good selection of traditional pub food is on offer at the **Buck Inn** in the neighbouring village of Flixton. Telephone 01986 892382.

THE WALK

Leave the car park and turn left passing some farm buildings on the right. Pass through a gate to gain access to pasture ahead. Cross the latter (on a permissive path) and head slightly left towards a kissing gate. Go through the gate and turn left to join **Debbs Lane**. The lane shortly starts to descend a shallow valley.

At the bottom, turn left to enter a long rectangular field of pasture, keeping to the right edge as you go to the other side of the field.

Deep in the heart of rural countryside you will soon be aware of the peaceful surroundings, well away from the noise of vehicular traffic and every day stresses. The meadows here are the remnants of a medieval deer park. Trees include oak, beech and 500-year-old pollarded hornbeams.

If you have binoculars with you

take a good look round. You may be able to spot some of the birds that are listed on a board outside the entrance to Bateman's Barn.

Pass through another kissing gate into more pasture. Stay on the right edge to reach a large oak tree with an enclosure of more trees just beyond it. Turn right through a kissing gate with directions '**To The Minster**'. Follow the grassy path to discover the ruins in front.

The minster was once described as 'one of the most enigmatic and romantic ruins in England'. But why does it stand in such splendid isolation? Some historians suggest it may have been an earthwork of Roman origin. On the other hand, the local area was of ecclesiastical importance when Bishops of Norwich lived at South Elmham Hall. Tantalisingly, it's also thought that the remains may belong to Suffolk's 'lost' Anglo-Saxon cathedral. A nearby interpretation board provides some clues on the Minster's history.

Drive and Stroll

Bateman's Barn was once the stables

 ④

Retrace steps previously taken through the kissing gate and turn right. Follow the hedge for about another 250 yards. Turn left through a kissing gate and head up an ascending field edge path with a hedge on the right.

 ⑤

Turn right at the top of the field into

Mill Lane. After about 30 yards turn left and follow the path to reach a T-junction of paths. Turn left here and later pass some buildings at **Old Hall Farm**. Carry straight on to eventually meet a minor road at **Frog Hall**. Turn left and continue along the road back to your start point.

PLACES OF INTEREST NEARBY

On the B1062, just outside Bungay is the **Norfolk and Suffolk Aviation Museum** where admission is free, with donations welcomed. Telephone: 01986 896644.

2 | Wenhaston

Wenhaston is a peaceful village

The Walk 3 miles ⏱1½ hours
Map OS Explorer No 231 Southwold & Bungay (GR 425574)

How to get there

Wenhaston lies some 3 miles south-east of Halesworth and 6 miles west of Southwold. From Ipswich take the A12 and turn left just before reaching Blythburgh onto the signposted road to Wenhaston (about 2 miles). **Parking**: Wenhaston village hall.

Drive and Stroll

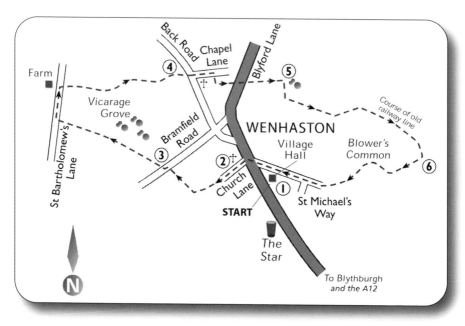

Introduction

Wenhaston is a quiet village nestling on the edge of the picturesque Blyth valley. The mostly grassy footpaths at time of walking were in good condition, in fact, a pleasure to walk. The route takes you out into the countryside, past remnants of heath and commons, back through the village along what is known as the narrow way. Part of the walk follows the line of the old Halesworth-Southwold railway. Apart from the good walking, what attracts visitors to this village is the impressive doom painting in St Peter's church. The village has a very active community, with a modern village hall that houses a post office.

The Star

This old-fashioned pub stands beside the road just before you reach Wenhaston. Walkers are assured of a warm welcome, with the opportunity of a banter with some of the locals. Food is available at reasonable prices. On offer is a selection of sandwiches with baguettes to order. Home-made soups feature on the menu, along with favourites such as ham, egg and chips, shepherd's pie and steak dishes. There's a selection of Adnams ales to choose from plus a weekly guest beer. Tea and coffee is also served. Children are welcomed here. Telephone: 01502 478240.

THE WALK

Leave the village hall car park and cross to **Church Lane** nearby.

If you want to look around St Peter's church, do so now – at this stage you shouldn't have any mud on your boots! In the north aisle is The Doom or Last Judgement painting. It's thought the painting, on boards with the great rood and its supporting figures attached, was made by a monk from Blythburgh Priory around 1500. Its purpose was to present a mostly illiterate congregation with a stark challenge: are you going to heaven or hell? Some 50 years later the boards were whitewashed over. In 1892 when the chancel was being restored, the boards were taken down and thrown out into the churchyard. That night it rained hard, washing off the covering and revealing the treasure we see today.

Go past **Church Cottages** and continue ahead to reach a path that runs between a paddock fence and a hedge. Bear right just beyond some sports facilities on the left and shortly go right again along the side of a rail fence. Ignore a path going left and continue ahead to reach the **Bramfield** road in front.

Cross the road and swing right with a hedge on the right. Pass **Vicarage Grove** ahead and carry on to finally reach **St Bartholomew's Lane**. Turn right here, pass **St Bartholomew's Farm** and in about 200 yards turn right at a field entrance. Make your way back in the direction of **Wenhaston**, with a hedge on the left. Later on, the path passes between trees and along an old earth lane with high banks.

Cross **Back Road** to join **Chapel Lane** opposite and shortly pass the **Wesleyan Methodist chapel** dated 1835. Follow the tarmac lane downhill and turn left opposite **Coles Croft**. Pass close to a cottage on the left to enter a low-lying area and later emerge beside **Blyford Lane**. Cross the road, turn left to cross a stile in the fence on the right. Follow a grassy path on a bank and turn right at the far end. Continue on a field break path and swing left beside an oak tree. Carry on to cross another field on a similar break path. Pass through a gap at the boundary, follow the path to an opening and afterwards pass a cottage beside a track on the left.

In front, across the Blyth valley, is a large housing complex. It stands on the site of the old Blythburgh hospital, built in 1766 as a workhouse.

Turn right beside a gate and stile onto a field edge path. This is a permissive path and access is courtesy of the landowner.

You are now walking along the track bed of the former Southwold-Halesworth railway, a distance of almost 9 miles. The station at Wenhaston was situated half a mile from the village, much to the displeasure of local residents. Opened in 1879 and closed in 1929, the narrow-gauge railway ran on a single three feet wide track. Towards the end of its life the eccentric railway with its open-top carriages became the subject of much ridicule. It finally gave way to buses that covered the distance in a much faster time. In recent years attempts have been made to revive the line as part of a local transport system.

The two church towers seen in the middle distance belong to Blyford on the left and on the right Blythburgh, often referred to as the 'Cathedral of the Marshes'.

 ⑥

Soon the path passes through an avenue of oak trees to reach a

Notice the bird box on Wenhaston's attractive village sign

galvanised gate. Go through the gate to join a rising stony track. Pass **Blower's Common** at the top and ignore paths going left and right. Continue along a footway, pass **St Michael's Way** and later emerge beside the village hall car park.

PLACES OF INTEREST NEARBY

Walpole Old Chapel, on the B1117, west of Halesworth, looks like an old Suffolk timber-framed farmhouse. However, the building is an important Nonconformist chapel. The interior layout looks much the same as it did when congregations first met here during the Civil War period. Telephone: 01986 798308.

3 | Eye

The church of St Peter & St Paul and the Guildhall in Eye

The Walk 2 miles 🕐 1 hour (allow more for sight-seeing)
Map OS Explorer No 230 Diss & Harleston (GR 144738)

How to get there

The town of Eye lies 21 miles north of Ipswich and 5 miles south of Diss. From Ipswich or the Norwich direction take the A140. Turn off beside The Bull Auberge restaurant at Yaxley to join the B1117. As you approach Eye, turn left just before the first road junction and go left into Cross Street and the car park. **Parking**: Cross Street free car park where there are public toilets.

Drive and Stroll

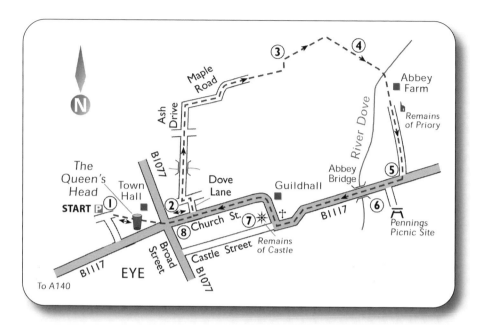

Introduction

Early settlers here encountered an area deep in swamp, which on occasions could only be reached by boat. Unsurprisingly, the name of Eye is derived from the Angle-Saxon 'aye' – a term denoting a slightly raised site surrounded by marsh that could in severe weather become an island. Nowadays, as you will discover on the walk, independent Eye may be considered as unfashionable, not moving with times but arguably all the better for it. Shops, with their unmodernised fronts – a throw-back to the 1950s perhaps – nevertheless provide a wide range of goods and services to their customers. Walk through the town's historic streets and periphery, climb the castle ruins, visit the magnificent parish church and, pardon the expression, you will receive an eyeful of Eye.

The Queen's Head

Once upon a time there were some dozen public houses in Eye. Now the Queen's Head, a pink-washed, half-timbered pub near the start of the walk, is the sole remainder. In the bar area expect to find locals with a broad Suffolk accent mingling with shoppers from the town's agricultural hinterlands. Daily specials listed on the menu board include the likes of fish and chips, quiche, chicken korma and tuna pasta bake. Meals are served in a small restaurant, complete with low beams and a large fireplace at the rear of the pub. For desserts there is a choice of popular favourites such as apple crumble, spotted dick and chocolate pudding. Adnams is on offer here along with a choice of other beers and ales. Telephone: 01379 870153.

THE WALK

 ①

From the car park go past the **Queen's Head** and pass the Victorian town hall on the left.

Eye attained borough status and at one time sent two representatives to Parliament, reduced to one by the Reform Act of 1832. The railway came and went, leaving the town with little industry and partial economic decline.

 ②

Cross **Broad Street** to join **Church Street** in front. After about another 120 yards, turn left into **Dove Lane**. At the next junction, turn left and then take the next turning right. Follow the descending road, cross a bridge over a watercourse and head up the other side. Cross an estate road, proceed along **Ash Drive** and turn right. Quickly swing left into **Maple Road**, cross onto a footway and follow it round a corner. At the far end, pass between barriers which lead into a small parking area, and head towards a stile beside a field edge.

 ③

Look for a cross-field path and walk towards the far side of the field.

Away to the right the tall tower of Eye church can be seen soaring above the countryside, more of which later. Walking amongst arable fields with the town in the background, gives you some idea of Eye's relative isolation from neighbouring communities.

 ④

Exit the field and join a descending field edge path with a hedge on the right. Keep forward on a section of concreted path and soon cross the infant **River Dove**, little more than a slow moving stream here. Cross another stile with **Abbey Farm** on the left. Continue ahead to pass the remains of an 11th-century priory, half-hidden in the gardens of the farmhouse.

An information panel beside the path gives a short history of the priory's rise and fall.

 ⑤

Turn right when you reach the B1117 and proceed along the road.

Drive and Stroll

Look left for the road leading to Pennings picnic site, handy if you wish to use the picnic tables there. This is also a good area for youngsters to have a run around.

Cross the **Abbey Bridge** and pass over the **Dove** again. Where the road bends left, cross with the utmost care and pass through a small metal gate to enter the churchyard. Continue ahead to reach the front entrance of **St Peter** and **St Paul's** parish church.

You can't fail to be impressed by the soaring flushwork of the 100 ft high tower, making it one of the finest in East Anglia. With few apparent local benefactors, it's said that finance for construction was provided by the 'people themselves'. Inside the church there is a treasure trove of items worth exploring. Located next door is the substantially timber-framed

Guildhall, now a private house.
If you want to visit the castle mound, turn left and then bear right into Castle Hill. The entrance to the ruins is on the right. Climb to the top of the castle built after the Norman Conquest and get a panoramic view of the town's irregular-shaped street pattern and the countryside beyond. The keep on the summit is that of a 19th-century folly which was destroyed in a storm during the 1960s.

Bear right to rejoin **Church Street**.

Beards café and delicatessen on the right offers tea or coffee and a range of light refreshments.

When you eventually reach the end of **Church Street**, cross straight over and retrace your steps back to **Cross Street** car park.

PLACES OF INTEREST NEARBY

South of Eye, at Debenham, is **Carters Teapot Pottery**. Here, you can watch the highly skilled staff producing collectable teapots. There is a pottery shop to browse in, as well as a tearoom that serves tea, naturally enough, from a Carter's teapot. Telephone: 01728 860475.

4 | Sizewell

Boats on the beach at Sizewell

The Walk 2½ miles 🕐 1½ hours
Map OS Explorer No 212 Woodbridge & Saxmundham (GR 475240)

How to get there

The hamlet of Sizewell lies about 25 miles north-east of Ipswich and 8 miles south of Southwold. Take the A12 and just north of Farnham turn right onto the A1094. Pass through Snape and in another 2 miles turn left onto the B1069. Follow the latter to Leiston and then join a road signposted to Sizewell (about 2 miles). **Parking**: Pay and display car park at Sizewell beach.

Drive and Stroll

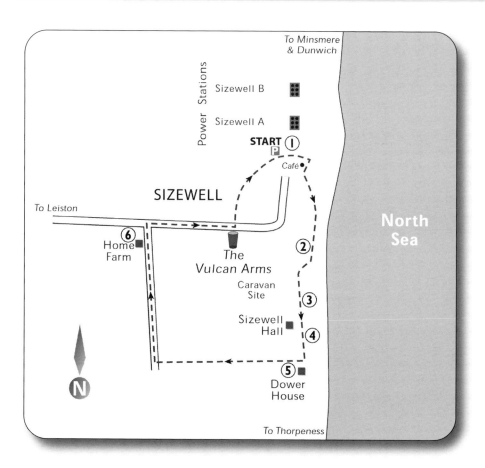

Introduction

The small coastal settlement of Sizewell often grabs the headlines due to publicity surrounding the two (and later possibly three) nuclear power stations sited there. There's little else to Sizewell village apart from Sizewell Hall, farmsteads, caravan park, pub, beach café and a sprinkling of cottages. The scenic walk takes you amongst sand dunes and along the cliff top where there are fine views of the beach and sea. Part of the walk follows the Suffolk Coast and Heaths Path, which starts at Cattawade near Manningtree and ends at Lowestoft, a distance of about 50 miles. The featured walk below can be extended with a route progressing through an area known as the Sizewell Belts and Kenton Hills. You can obtain leaflets with a map and walking instructions from the Vulcan Arms.

Sizewell Beach Café

Ideally situated beside the beach and access road, this small friendly café offers visitors a good range of refreshments, including tea, coffee, soft drinks and a selection of ice cream. Light bites include snacks and sandwiches. If it's something more substantial you're after, try a full English breakfast, fish and chips or a salad. You can sit and eat at outside tables, ideal if the sun is shining. The café often gets quite crowded with walkers, bikers and a steady stream of tourists, especially at weekends and bank holidays. Check in advance for opening times, currently Wednesday – Sunday 9 am to 5 pm Telephone: 01728 830282. There is a public toilet block almost next door. If you fancy an alcoholic beverage, try the nearby Vulcan Arms pub. Telephone: 01728 830748.

THE WALK

Leave the beach car park to join a stretch of boardwalk that passes beside the toilet block on the right and then heads onto the shingle beach. Turn right and walk amongst the sand dunes.

On the vegetated beach look out for plants such as sea kale and yellow-horned poppies that flower in the summer. Looking north beyond the two power stations is the RSPB reserve at Minsmere. Further on are the white coastguard cottages at Dunwich. On a clear day you may be able to spot the inland lighthouse at Southwold.

The two offshore platforms are used to offload equipment for delivery to the power stations. The beach is a popular spot for seasoned anglers, often seen with their lines cast out to sea. Usually a fishing boat or two is winched up on the beach.

During the mid-18th century, smugglers known as the Hadleigh Gang were active along this stretch of wild and rugged coastline known as the Sizewell Gap. They brought ashore contraband goods such as tea, spirits and tobacco, hotly pursued by excise men and dragoon soldiers. Horse-drawn carts were a common sight on the beach, taking the contraband for hiding in pre-arranged locations.

Veer slightly right through the dunes and continue up a sloping bank.

Nearby is a black and white building known as The Watch House, formerly a lookout for coastguards. In 2004 it was awarded a Grade II listing because of its special historic and architectural interest. Coastguards

Drive and Stroll

Sizewell A power station

at one time lived in other adjacent black-boarded cottages. The nearby wooden pole was used to launch rockets for sea rescue practice.

↪ ③

Go past the clubhouse of the **Cliff House caravan site** and just before reaching a **Suffolk Coast and Heaths** waymark sign, climb up some steps amongst an area of brambles and bracken to reach the top of a shallow cliff. Turn left and carry on ahead along the cliff top, shortly going under the bridge of **Sizewell Hall**.

The impressive Hall, once thatched, belongs to the local Ogilvie family. Incidentally, it was Stuart Ogilvie who created neighbouring Thorpeness at the turn of the 20th century as part of a fantasy children's home with a theme of Peter Pan. The Hall was almost burnt down in 1920 but was later rebuilt. Nowadays it's used as a Christian Conference Centre.

↪ ④

Keep walking south, in the direction of **Thorpeness** village, until you reach an area of large concrete blocks; they were placed here during the Second World War as a first line of defence to deter any seaborne invasion by enemy forces.

Turn right here and walk inland through the trees, later passing a pair of thatched gatehouses. Pass through a gap in a rail fence to the drive from **Dower House**. Shortly turn right onto a track, which later develops into a surfaced road, following a boundary wall. Continue along the tree-lined road, passing

the metal gates of **Sizewell Hall** as you go.

After passing some farm buildings at **Home Farm**, the road brings you to a T-junction. Turn right here onto a footway beside the **Leiston-Sizewell** road to later reach the **Vulcan Arms** car park. Opposite the latter, cross the road, go over a stile and make your way across a grassy area back to your starting point. Alternatively, keep following the road that brings you back to the café and car park.

PLACES OF INTEREST NEARBY

Northwards along the coast at **Dunwich** is a museum, located in the rooms of a small cottage. It contains an impressive model of the town that disappeared into the sea. There is also a good display of local art and natural history. Tel: 01728 648796.

5 Aldeburgh

The 16th-century Moot Hall at Aldeburgh

The Walk 3 or 4 miles ⏲ 2 hours or 3 hours.
Map OS Explorer No 212 Woodbridge & Saxmundham Aldeburgh & Framlingham (GR 465559)

How to get there

From the A12 a few miles south of Saxmundham take the A1094 to Aldeburgh. Carry on through the town centre following the road south to eventually reach an unmade road adjacent to Fort Green at Slaughden. **Parking**: Pay and display car park at Fort Green, south of Aldeburgh town. Alternatively, leave the car beside the rough gravel track (free) as others tend to do.

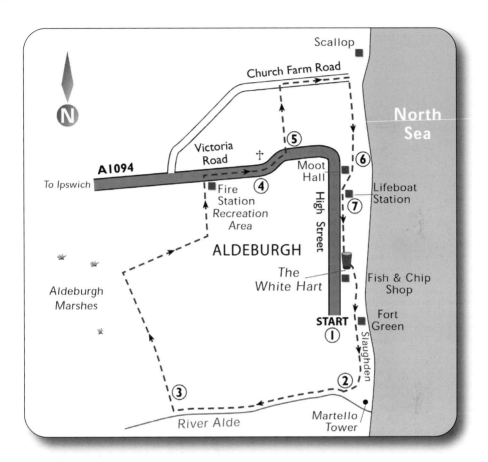

Introduction

Aldeburgh is an historic port and former borough which once sent two representatives to Parliament, later to be disenfranchised by the Reform Act of 1832. The walk starts at neighbouring Slaughden, once a flourishing fishing and boat-building village. The well-known poet George Crabbe, whose father was a local customs official, was born here in 1754. The village eventually fell victim to the surging North Sea and gradually disappeared under the waves. Nowadays only the Martello tower and yacht club remain. Later on, the route takes you over the lonely marshes where you may encounter little more than grazing cattle. There's a chance to take a peep inside the interesting church of St Peter and St Paul and afterwards, view a controversial metal scallop. The return leg passes the historic Moot Hall and the lifeboat station.

Drive and Stroll

The Aldeburgh Fish and Chip Shop and the White Hart Inn

There are a number of pubs, restaurants and cafés in Aldeburgh to suit every taste. I've chosen a couple of establishments that are recommended for service and value. Family-run since 1967, the fish and chip shop at No 226 High Street is reckoned to be one of the finest in East Anglia. Expect queuing such is its popularity. Afterwards take your meal and eat it on the adjacent beach but beware of swooping gulls! Telephone: 01728 452250. If you prefer eating indoors, try the Upper Deck restaurant in the High Street run by the same company.

The White Hart pub at 222 High Street almost rubs shoulders with the fish shop. Although it consists of only one small room and often gets crowded, the pub generates plenty of atmosphere, mostly with a nautical flavour. No hot food but a wide choice of sandwiches, including popular smoked cheese and different fillings. Beers served include Adnams and other guest ales. Telephone: 01728 453205.

THE WALK

Leave the **Fort Green car park** and turn left to join a broad gravel track.

Ahead is the outline of a Martello Tower completed in 1810 to repel the threat of a Napoleonic invasion. Sited between the River Alde and the North Sea, this particular tower is the most northerly of a defensive network along the east coast. Most towers are circular in shape but this one consists of four circles joined together, like the shape of a four-leaf clover. Nowadays the property belongs to the Landmark Trust and you can stay in it as a holiday home.

Just before reaching the **Slaughden**

sailing club yard, turn right beside a finger post to join a narrow sandy path.

On the left is the picturesque River Alde, making its way to Orford where it becomes the River Ore. The tall aerials seen in the distance are those used to transmit the BBC's World Service.

Where the path starts to curve left, turn right down some steps and cross a watercourse. Continue on a broad path through the marshes and shortly ignore a path going right. Soon the path starts to wind its way back towards the town. Turn left when you reach a brick boundary wall and continue on a surfaced path. Pass some allotments and shortly reach a recreation area. After passing the

26

The scallop sculpture on the beach at Aldeburgh

town's fire station, turn right into **Victoria Road**. *(If you wish to take the 3-mile option, continue along Victoria Road to eventually reach either the High Street or sea front. Turn right here and make your way back to the start point.)*

 ④

To follow the 4 mile route, when you reach the parish church, cross the road to find a path running through the churchyard.

Inside the church you'll find memorials to two of Aldeburgh's famous sons: a window in memory of composer Benjamin Britten (1913-76), and a bust of poet George Crabbe (1754-1832). You

will find Britten's grave and headstone, along with those of Peter Pears and Imogen Holst, in the churchyard.

 ⑤

Continue through the churchyard, pass through a small gate, ignoring a path and road going right. Carry on downhill to meet the junction with **Church Farm Road**. Turn right and head towards the beach. Cross the road and turn right again to join a footway.

Away to the left is the controversial sculpture of a metal scallop erected in honour of Benjamin Britten in 2003. The sculpture has frequently been daubed in paint by vandals

Drive and Stroll

and arguments rage over its particular siting on the shingle beach.

 ⑥

Continue on the surfaced path and pass the historic 16th-century **Moot Hall**.

When it was built, the Hall stood in what was then the town centre surrounded by narrow streets. However, due to the encroaching North Sea, it now stands perilously close to the beach. This fine timber-framed building was originally the town hall and still functions as

such. A climb up the wooden staircase takes you to the council chamber and museum room that displays artefacts of local interest. Telephone: 01728 454666.

 ⑦

Join the **Crag Path** ahead and walk beside the beach, passing the lifeboat station and an old lookout point – now an art gallery – as you go. If you want to visit the fish shop or pub, turn right by **King Street car park** and go left into the **High Street**. Otherwise stay on the path and return to your point of departure.

PLACES OF INTEREST NEARBY

The original control tower at **Parham Airfield** near Framlingham (occupied by the US military during the Second World War) has been restored, and is now a museum with exhibits including engines and other artefacts, and also memorabilia relating to the British Resistance Organisation. Tel: 01728 621373.

6 Easton

Easton Farm Park passed on the walk

The Walk 3 miles ⏲ 2 hours – longer if stopping at Easton Farm Park
Map OS Explorer No 212 Woodbridge & Saxmundham (GR 283595)

How to get there

The village of Easton lies 3 miles south of Framlingham and 7 miles north of Woodbridge. From the A12 at Lower Hacheston take the B1116 north towards Framlingham. After ¼ mile turn left on Easton Road and follow the signposted minor roads to Easton village (about 3 miles). **Parking**: The small car park in front of Almond Tree Cottage, about 60 yards from the pub.

Drive and Stroll

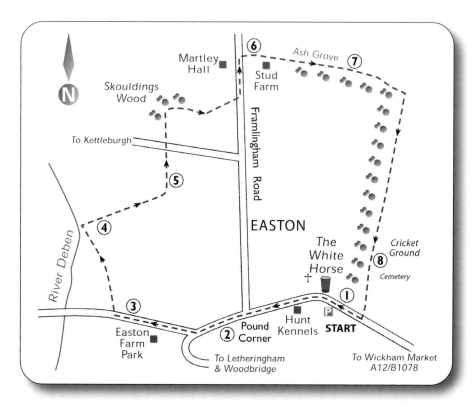

Introduction

When the Duke of Hamilton (and his family, 1780 to 1919) created his Easton Hall estate, he decided on an unusual means to enclose it all. Instead of using a conventional thick hedge or deep ditch, the Duke constructed what's called a crinkle-crankle wall. You'll find long stretches of the wall as you walk around the estate boundary, including a section mortared onto the tower of All Saints church. Easton Hall no longer survives – it was demolished in the 1920s. The walk passes the entrance to Easton Farm Park, a firm favourite with children and home of the famous Suffolk Punches. Later on, a horsey theme is continued with horses present in paddocks attached to a local stud farm.

The White Horse

Can there be a more attractive entrance to a Suffolk pub, with roses round the front door and a garden blooming with flowers? Little wonder the floral displays at this former 16th-century coaching inn make it one of Suffolk's prettiest pubs. Dishes such as sausage, ham and chips, chicken Kiev, omelettes and home-made soups are firm favourites here with walkers. Haddock and chips, broccoli bake in a leek and Stilton sauce, stir fry and pasta are among other dishes to be found on the comprehensive menu. The pub also does a Sunday roast, plus afternoon teas and cakes. Telephone: 01728 746456.

THE WALK

Leave the car park and turn left to continue on a footway. Pass the **White Horse pub** and reach the triangular green, with the village sign depicting a pack of foxhounds standing almost in front of **All Saints church**.

Just around the corner are the kennels of the Easton Harriers Hunt. Despite fears that the 48 foxhounds would disappear when the Hunting Act took effect, they still remain boarded here and appear regularly at local meets during the autumn and winter months.

Soon you will see the first real stretch of a crinkle-crankle wall, which is often referred to as a Serpentine wall. The curving line apparently gives added strength without the need for buttresses. It's the longest wall of its kind in Britain and it's said that it took a father and son a lifetime to build. Goodness knows how many thousands of bricks were made to complete the wall. They were

probably fired locally, possibly on the estate itself.

Look right for an unusual circular shaped cottage standing back with a large central block chimney stack. Built for an estate worker, perhaps it was another example of the Duke's efforts to beautify the village.

Swing left by the road junction at **Pound Corner** and later ignore a road going left to **Letheringham**. Stay on the road to reach the entrance to **Easton Farm Park**.

The buildings inside the park were built as a model farm in about 1870 by the Duke of Hamilton. As you pass by, look in adjacent driveway paddocks and you may see some resplendent Suffolk Punch horses, possibly with foals.

Carry on along the road passing a tiled barn set back on the right. Continue ahead for about another 500 yards to reach the bottom of a hill. Turn right as indicated by a fingerpost and continue along a broad grassy path with a hedge on the left.

Look left through the hedge gaps and you will see Hoo church across the meadows. The church was used for burial scenes in the classic film 'Akenfield'.

 ④

Continue ahead and walk beside the infant river **Deben**, almost hidden from view and choked in places by dense undergrowth. After passing a thin line of willow trees, leave the path and turn right to take a gently rising path, with a hedge on the left.

The river originates in mid Suffolk at Debenham and, after meandering through villages in the Deben valley, it finally enters the North Sea at Bawdsey.

 ⑤

At the top end turn left onto an access track and proceed to reach the road ahead. Turn left, walk along the road for about 100 yards and take the next turning right. A field edge path brings you to the edge of **Skouldings Wood**. Turn right here and continue ahead to with the wood on the left. Go under some power lines and later reach

the **Framlingham** road. Turn left and continue along the road for another 300 yards. Turn right just in front of a post box positioned beside the road.

 ⑥

Cross a sleeper bridge and carry on between a paddock fence on the left and a hedge on right.

On the right is a stud farm. Horses can often be seen exercising in the yard and grazing in nearby paddocks.

 ⑦

Enter the next field and continue to the far corner. Turn right onto another field edge path with the boundary wall on the right, noting the gaps and want of restoration as you go past.

The Easton cricket field will shortly appear on the left. The club celebrated its centenary in 2006. For a small village the facilities, including a spacious pavilion, look quite impressive.

 ⑧

After passing a cemetery on the left the path descends to meet the road in **Easton**. Turn right and the car park is just ahead on the left.

The crinkle-crankle wall in Easton

PLACES OF INTEREST NEARBY

Framlingham Castle, with its 13 towers still intact, looks almost the same as when it was built in the 12th century. From the wall-walk, reached by a spiral staircase, there are excellent views over the reed-fringed mere and the town of Framlingham. Tel: 01728 685789.

7 Newbourne

The Fox Inn at Newbourne

The Walk 3 miles ⏱ 2 hours
Map OS Explorer 197 Ipswich, Felixstowe & Harwich (GR 274432)

How to get there

Newbourne village lies about 4 miles south of Woodbridge. From Ipswich or Felixstowe leave the A14 at the Bucklesham junction and join the A12. At the next roundabout, Brightwell Corner, take the signposted Waldringfield road. Follow the road to Waldringfield Heath and turn right at the crossroads. In about another 1½ miles you'll find the nature reserve entrance on the right, just before reaching a T-junction. **Parking**: The small car park at Newbourne Springs Nature Reserve.

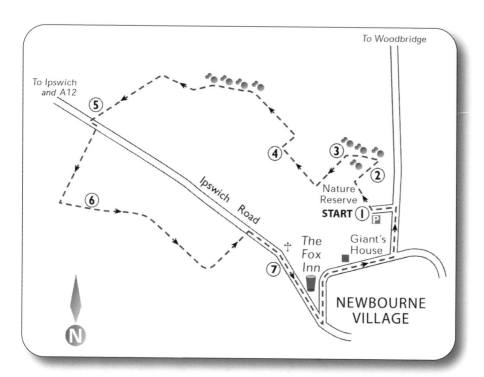

Introduction

A large part of this walk takes place in a steep-sided wooded valley, an unusual feature for Suffolk. The site belongs to Anglian Water Services and is managed for wildlife conservation by the Suffolk Wildlife Trust. Until the early 1980s natural springs from within the nature reserve supplied the surrounding area with water. As a result, you'll find stretches of boardwalk and bridges to carry you over some of the more marshy areas. Most of the paths inside are permissive and are often cleared by volunteer work parties.

The village is well known for two brothers who once lived here, George and Meadows Page, both over 7 ft tall and often referred to as the local giants. You can visit their grave and later pass the Giants' House where they lived.

The Fox Inn

The pub stands beside the road in the village and is well-known for its attractive floral displays, especially during the summer season. Main courses include a choice of roasts, chicken, steak and kidney pudding, gammon steak and lasagne. Specials here are home-made steak pies made

Drive and Stroll

exclusively for the pub. If you fancy something lighter, sandwiches and ploughman's are also served. There's a wide selection of desserts on offer. Drinks include Adnams and other guest ales and beers. You can eat in or outside on picnic tables. The Fox is quite a busy pub and booking is recommended. Telephone: 01473 736307.

THE WALK

From the small car park go through a kissing gate beside the old pumping station to enter the reserve. After a straight stretch of path, you start walking along a narrow timber walkway with swampy conditions underfoot. Small bridges take you over a boggy area beside a shallow stream amongst reedbeds and alder carr.

Note the old green water-gauging machine on the left as you pass through. The streams contain watercress, mint and marsh marigold flowers. Woodland birds such as woodpeckers are seen and heard here. If you are lucky you might hear the unmistakable song of a nightingale, especially during a May evening.

Turn right where the boardwalk ends and quickly starts again. Do not deviate from the now public path that continues through areas of bracken and nettles. The undulating path continues to skirt the steep slopes of the valley side where

oak and ash trees form a high canopy.

Turn left about 10 yards before reaching a stile ahead. Pass down some steps in the bank to join another stretch of boardwalk which passes between trees and bracken and leads to a broad grassy path. With a wooden fence either side of the path, go sharp right through a gap in the fence and continue on a rising path through a thin belt of trees.

Follow the path to an open field and swing right to skirt the edge of a sloping field. Curve left at the bottom and continue beside the reserve. Just as you think the path is never ending, a rise in the ground suddenly brings you to a three-finger signpost positioned at the boundary. Turn left and carry on beside a rising field edge path with a hedge on the left.

Look over your shoulder and in the distance is the British Telecom research station at Martlesham.

Reach the **Ipswich** road in front and

The old pumping station at the entrance to the nature reserve

turn left. Go quickly right to pass through a kissing gate and a track leading to **Lower House**. Although the entrance is marked private, the public right of way runs beside the track. After about 250 yards turn left over a stile into an arable field and continue through successive fields with a hedge on the left.

The light soil here is very conducive to vegetable growing and you may encounter large mobile irrigation equipment spraying the fields during periods of drought.

Remnants of greenhouses still exist en route. During the late 1930s and onwards there were acres of them. They formed part of the Land Settlement Association, a government-sponsored scheme to assist out-of-work miners to produce and sell fruit and vegetables. Most of the scheme was wound up in the 1980s, mainly due to costs and over production.

Just after the broad sandy path starts to descend, look left for a fingerpost and kissing gate. Pass through the latter, passing a working area of pots and trays with greenhouses beyond. Climb a stile in the corner, bear left and continue to the Ipswich Road in front. Turn right along a path on top of a roadside bank and climb some

Drive and Stroll

steps at the far end. **St Mary's church** will shortly appear on the left.

Inside the churchyard are the remains of a remarkable man, George Page. Along with his brother Meadows, they became known as the local giants. George died in 1870. He stood 7 ft 7 ins tall in his bare feet with Meadows a few inches shorter. Both acquired considerable fame with a travelling fair where they were exhibited in front of curious onlookers. Meadows

continued to tour and died later in 1917. George's grave and a faded headstone can be found by the eastern side of the church path.

Carry on to the road junction in front and turn left to enter **The Street**. Pass the **Fox pub** and follow the road to pass the **Giants' House** where the Page brothers lived. At the next road junction turn left onto the **Woodbridge** road with the car park ahead on the left.

PLACES OF INTEREST NEARBY

Buttrums Mill at Woodbridge (8 miles to the north) is the tallest surviving windmill in Suffolk. It dates from around 1836, and last worked in 1928. The fully restored brick-built tower has four large, shuttered sails. Details of the mill's history are displayed on the ground floor. Tel: 01473 264755.

8 Nacton and Levington

Nacton's foreshore

The Walk 3 miles ⏱1½ hours
Map OS Explorer No 197 Ipswich, Felixstowe & Harwich (GR 220391)

How to get there

From the A14/A12 interchange south-east of Ipswich, follow the A1156 towards Ipswich. In half a mile turn left to Nacton. Go straight through the village and follow the brown signs for Nacton Picnic Site. Just past the gates of Orwell School turn right to join a narrow road that heads directly to the picnic site. **Parking**: A choice of three – a small one on the left and two others further down the access road.

Drive and Stroll

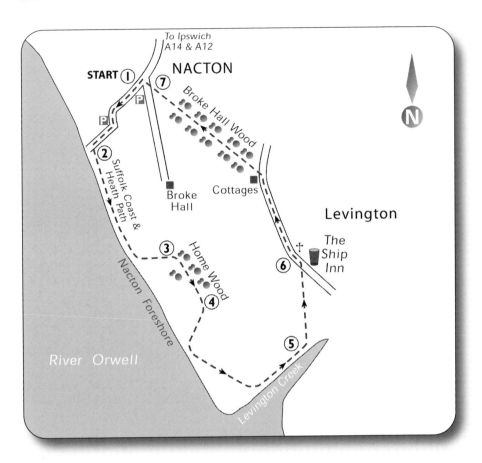

Introduction

Walking is the ideal way of exploring this delightful route that is hidden well away from vehicular traffic. The walk contains a mixture of river path, marshland, deciduous woodland and small lagoons. Bring a pair of binoculars to view small wading birds, their beaks probing for molluscs and crustaceans on exposed mud flats. The period between October and March is a good time for birdwatching when there are many species wintering along the Orwell estuary.

The Ship Inn

An uphill stretch over pasture finally brings you to the Ship Inn at Levington where you can relax in an ambience of things nautical with picturesque views over the marshes. A snug and cosy atmosphere welcomes you in this 14th-century pub, along with a cheery log fire during the winter months. An extensive menu offers choices such as home-made soups, liver and bacon, cold meat platter and a selection of steak and fish dishes. Drinks include Adnams and IPA. Telephone: 01473 659573

THE WALK

Leave the car park and continue to descend the tree-lined road. Pass through a staggered junction to finally arrive at the river foreshore, greeted by the gently lapping tide and smell of seaweed.

In front is the tidal river Orwell. When the tide recedes it exposes large areas of muddy ooze. Small wading birds such as redshank and dunlin can often be seen here probing the mud for submerged food. You can watch commercial ships navigating the narrow channel leading to the inland port of Ipswich. Situated on the opposite side of the river is the hamlet of Pin Mill, a popular sailing centre for dinghy enthusiasts and a mooring for Thames barges with their distinctive red sails.

Turn left to join the **Suffolk Coast and Heath path** and continue through a broad green picnic area – no tables but one or two benches. Bring a blanket on a summer's day and you can enjoy a pleasant picnic.

The imposing building over to the left is Broke Hall (now luxury flats). Sir Philip Bowes Vere Broke was born here in 1776 and later became a distinguished officer in the Royal Navy. He is best remembered for his command of the frigate HMS Shannon *and the defeat of the USS* Chesapeake *as it attempted to evade the blockade of Boston harbour on 1 June 1813. There is a memorial to Sir Philip in Nacton church.*

Continue on the sandy path that steadily rises and leads into **Home Wood**. Later on, fork left by a waymark sign.

Pause hereabouts to admire scenic views from the top of small cliffs overlooking the estuary.

Exit the wooded area and carry on with a hedge on the right. Shortly the village of **Levington** will come into view. Tall masts of yachts moored at **Levington Marina** are noticeable in the middle distance. At a T-junction of paths turn right. Go forward a few paces, climb some steps in the bank and turn left

Drive and Stroll

The tidal river Orwell at Nacton

to join the river wall that forms a protective barrier against the sea.

In front are brackish lagoons formed as a result of a breach in the sea wall during the disastrous east-coast floods of 1953.

Levington, you may recall, is often associated with a brand of peat and fertiliser. Fisons, who used to manufacture the product, once had a research station in the village.

Looming large to the right are gantry cranes belonging to the port of Felixstowe. The port is continually expanding and nowadays is the largest port in the country to handle container traffic.

You may come across birds such as finches and linnets – their red *and white tail feathers showing as they flit between clumps of gorse bushes.*

 (5)

Follow the well-worn path past a series of lagoons, reed beds and marsh to reach a mature hedge on the left. Just beyond the start of the hedge, break left through a gap into a field of pasture. Follow the long rising path and bear right at the top to arrive in front of the **Ship Inn**.

 (6)

Turn left onto a footway at **Church Lane** passing **All Saints church**. Pass a small cannon by the roadside and stay on the road for next 400 yards where it shortly goes downhill. Just beyond **East Lodge Cottages** turn left by a bridleway sign to enter **Broke Hall Wood**.

The well-worn narrow path passes through a boggy area, often churned up by horses' hoofs. Within the wood there are fine specimens of young and mature trees, including maple and sycamore. Bluebells and other wild flowers can often be found in *season. Sunshine, however, is often restricted from breaking through by the high canopy of trees.*

Exit the wood and emerge onto the road. Cross over the latter, passing the entrance to **Broke Hall** on the left, and re-enter the picnic site. Carry straight on back to your point of departure.

PLACES OF INTEREST NEARBY

Sutton Hoo, by the banks of the river Deben, is sometimes referred to as 'page one of the history of England'. It is a unique and fascinating place. The exhibition hall contains a full-sized replica of the burial chamber of an Anglo-Saxon warrior king and his most treasured possessions. The site is located off the B1083 Woodbridge to Bawdsey Road. Follow signs from the A12. Tel: 01394 389700.

9 Felixstowe Ferry

Felixstowe Ferry

The Walk 6 miles ⏱ 3 hours.
Map OS Explorer 197 Ipswich, Felixstowe & Harwich (GR 329377)

How to get there

Felixstowe Ferry is 12 miles south-east of Ipswich. From Ipswich follow the A14 to the roundabout on the northern edge of the port of Felixstowe. Take the first exit A154 Candlet Road and later take the first exit at Grove Road roundabout. Proceed via the A1021 to the roundabout at Beatrice Avenue and take the third exit. Then take the first exit at High Road. From here, go straight into Cliff Road and shortly bear right to enter Ferry Road which takes you to Felixstowe Ferry. **Parking**: A small pay and display car park near the Ferry Café.

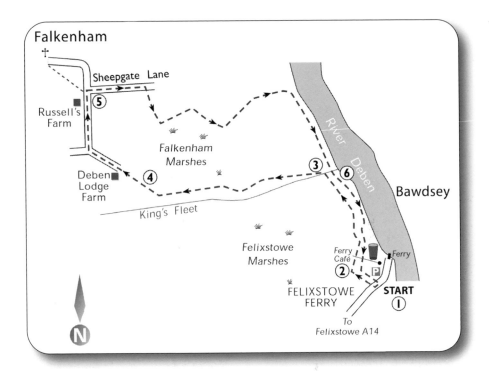

Introduction

This bracing walk starts from Felixstowe Ferry, a hamlet with secluded beaches and a scenic golf course. The lonely walk takes you across low-lying marshes and dykes, much of which have been drained and reclaimed to become cropped fields. Before walking a word of caution: the route in parts is quite isolated with little cover for protection from rain and wind. Therefore, if the weather is a bit iffy, be prepared to take waterproof clothing and stout footwear.

You can extend the walk by about half a mile to visit St Ethelbert's church at Falkenham. If you fancy exploring the other side of the river, a short ferry ride will take you over to Bawdsey Quay. Telephone: 01394 282173 for operating times.

Ferry Café

From the outside the café probably looks much the same as it was when it first opened in the 1930s. But then, the exterior is part of the café's charm and character. Amazingly it survived the disastrous east coast floods of

Drive and Stroll

1953. Step inside and you are greeted with a warm welcome from pleasant staff. The wood-panelled interior decor has a nautical flavour in keeping with the nearby Deben river and North Sea. Hung on the walls are fishing nets, miniature lanterns, paintings and other memorabilia of a maritime nature The café, which has achieved something of a cult status with visitors returning regularly from near and far, is renowned for its fish and chips. The likes of cod, plaice, haddock, mackerel and kippers are included on the menu. All-day breakfasts and a mug of tea are popular here, along with toasted teacakes and scones. The café gets exceptionally busy at weekends and during the summer season. You can eat inside or outside at trestle tables. There are public toilets situated across the road. Telephone: 01394 276305

THE WALK

Leave the car park and turn right onto a footway.

Across the way is the mouth of the river Deben, complete with sandbanks and swirling currents. Further along the coastline are two Martello towers built as a defensive measure against a possible Napoleonic invasion.

In a few paces, turn right again beside a fingerpost to join a narrow surfaced path, with a golf course on the left. Turn right through a springer stile and start walking along a stretch of river wall.

On the right-hand side, boats of all shapes and sizes and in all conditions are moored on the mud banks of the river Deben.

On a clear day you can see way over the lonely marshes and arable fields. The river Deben no longer carries commercial traffic and nowadays is crowded with sailing enthusiasts whose colourful craft can often be seen taking part in local yachting regattas.

Follow the river wall path on to another stile and shortly afterwards to a junction of paths marked with a three-finger footpath sign. Turn left down some steps in the bank to join a gravel track.

On the left is a stretch of water marked on the map as King's Fleet. The name is probably derived from the fleet of King Edward III who assembled over 40 ships here to sail for France and the Battle of Crècy. Anglers, in company with families of mute swans and cygnets, often frequent the water.

Ferry Café first opened in the 1930s

④

Stay on the track as it later starts to gently rise and pass **Deben Lodge Farm** where the track becomes surfaced. At the road junction ahead, turn right to shortly enter the village of **Falkenham**. Walk up the hill in front, passing **Russell's Farm** as you go.

If you wish to visit St Ethelbert's church turn left diagonally across the field towards the church which can be seen behind the trees on the other side of the field. The church is noted for its fine 15th-century tower panelled in split flint and stone. Inside there is a handsome single hammer-beam and arch-braced roof.

⑤

Turn right down **Sheepgate Lane** (marked Gosford Hall). After about 500 yards, just after passing a dead tree on the left, turn right by an electricity pole onto a broad grassy path. Soon veer left to continue beside a field edge with a ditch on the right. Carry on ahead and shortly cross a bridge and afterwards turn left by a marker post beside a water channel. Cross another wooden bridge and turn left, soon veering right to head in the direction of the river wall in front. Climb up a grassy bank and turn right at the top to continue along the wall.

The high ground here allows further

Drive and Stroll

fine views of the local landscape. To the left Ramsholt Quay can be seen in the distance along with Ramsholt Arms pub. The church with its Saxon round tower lies amongst the trees on the hill.

Further along to the right on the opposite bank of the river, partially hidden by trees, is Bawdsey Manor where Sir Robert Watson-Watt and his colleagues developed radar. Look closely and you'll see standing beside the road four detached houses, formerly married quarters belonging to RAF Bawdsey – note the missing other half!

Continue along the wall and retrace your steps to the car park.

Sometimes you will find freshly-landed fish, including sprats, prawns and dressed crab for sale at huts opposite the car park.

PLACES OF INTEREST NEARBY

Landguard Fort, Felixstowe. The last invasion of England was repelled here in 1667. Visitors today can explore a labyrinth of passageways, including casement rooms and gun positions, and discover some of the armament improvements made by Victorian engineers. Tel: 07749 695523.

10 Onehouse

By the water's edge at Lakeside

The Walk 3 miles ⏱1½ hours
Map OS Explorer No 211 Bury St Edmunds & Stowmarket (GR 027587)

How to get there

Onehouse village lies about 2 miles west of Stowmarket. From the Ipswich or Bury St Edmunds direction leave the A14 and take the A1120 to join the A1308 at the traffic lights and turn right. At the next roundabout bear left and head towards Combs Ford. Swing right into Combs Lane and turn right at the next road junction. Go over a bridge and shortly turn left beside a telephone box into Lower Road. Lakeside is just around the corner, opposite the Shepherd and Dog public house. **Parking**: Lakeside car park.

Drive and Stroll

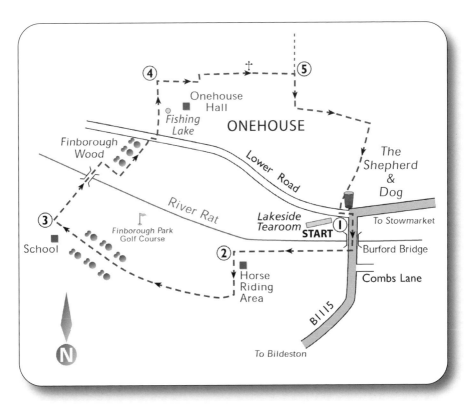

Introduction

Following considerable building expansion over recent years, there's more than one house in the village nowadays, if you see what I mean. Green fields currently separate Onehouse from the urban sprawl of Stowmarket, but for how much longer one might ask. The walk starts from the privately-owned Lakeside facility, an eight-acre area of lush meadowland and a large fishing lake. After hugging the riverside, the route follows undulating countryside in Finborough Park, where you need to watch out for flying golf balls. Later on, you pass Onehouse church with its unusual round tower, standing isolated amongst arable fields. The walk finishes literally beside the Shepherd and Dog pub with Lakeside just across the road.

Lakeside Tearoom

Visitors from near and wide flock to this popular tearoom that prides itself on serving an excellent brew of tea and coffee along with a varied selection of hot and cold food. During warm weather you have the choice of eating and relaxing outside with a view of the lake. Other facilities include sites for caravanning and camping, children's play areas and a large lake for fishing. The tearoom is open most of the year but telephone 01449 613770 for daily opening times.

THE WALK

Leave **Lakeside**, turn right and head towards the road junction in front. Turn right again and walk towards the narrow **Burford Bridge**. Be careful as there is a priority traffic system operating here. At the T-junction with Combs Lane ahead turn right into a field entrance and continue on a field edge path beside a rail fence. The path shortly runs beside the **river Rat** – a shortening of Rattlesden, a village that was an unlikely inland port during the Middle Ages. Cross two stiles and a bridge to arrive at an equestrian centre at **Home Farm**.

You'll see a number of horses and paddocks here, plus an area where you can learn to ride.

Continue ahead on a track that shortly curves left and steadily climbs. Nearing the top, turn right over a stile to enter **Finborough Park**. Bear left beside a golf green and head towards a fingerpost where you turn right. The way ahead passes through a thin belt of trees and beside some posts with a white circle.

The landscaped park is the home of Stowmarket golf club. As you walk through the park watch out for golfers and any flying golf balls. Both parties should acknowledge the other's presence and pause where appropriate.

The building away to the left is a former headquarters of an electricity board, nowadays occupied by St George's boarding school.

Turn right to join a partially surfaced path that quickly descends to a river bridge over the **Rat** at the bottom of a shallow valley. The river is now wider and deeper here. Carry on for another 75 yards and turn right to skirt **Finborough Wood** on the left. Cross **Lower Road** in front and maintain direction through an area of scrub to reach two private fishing lakes.

Beyond the lakes stands Onehouse Hall, parts of which date back to the 16th century, although the date of 1887 embedded in the wall suggests much later modernisation. The story goes that Elizabeth I stayed at the Hall during one of her royal progresses through the county.

Where the hedge finishes, turn right over a stile onto a grassy path and make your way towards the small church of **St John the Baptist**.

It's unusual to find a church locally with a round tower, most are found in the north of the county. Though the tower is possibly of Saxon origin, the church itself dates from the 14th century.

Continue along a track and where it later curves left, go through a gap beside the hedge and turn right onto a field edge path with a hedge on the right. Turn left at the boundary into the adjoining field and continue along a broad grass margin. Ignore paths going left and right and then proceed ahead on a path that acts as a field break. At the boundary turn right and follow a field edge path, later ignoring a path going left through a small sapling plantation. Stay on the path with a hedge on the left where it starts to descend and meets the **Shepherd and Dog** pub at the bottom. Cross the road and return to **Lakeside**.

PLACES OF INTEREST NEARBY

North-west of Onehouse, just off the A14, is the **Woolpit Museum**. It claims to be the smallest museum in Suffolk and inside you'll find items relevant to the local history of brickmaking, as well as early 20th-century kitchen equipment and photographs. Telephone: 01359 240822.

11 | Combs

The cricket ground at Combs

The Walk 3½ miles 🕐 2 hours
Map OS Explorer 211 Bury St Edmunds & Stowmarket (GR 042549)

How to get there

Combs village is one mile south of Stowmarket. From the Ipswich and Bury St Edmunds directions, leave the A14 at the junction to join the A1120. Continue to the A1308 and turn right at the traffic lights. Proceed to the next roundabout, bear left and carry on to Combs Ford. Turn left here to follow a minor road to Combs. The Gardeners Arms pub will be found in the village on the left-hand side. **Parking**: In the pub car park, with prior permission from the landlord.

Drive and Stroll

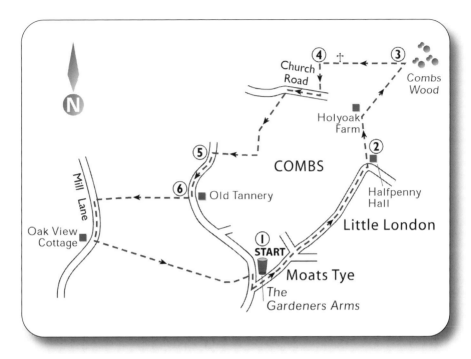

Introduction

This is one of my favourite walks. Well I would say that wouldn't I? It's part of my local patch. On the walk you'll find a terrain with plenty of slope and variety, along with historic places of interest to discover. St Mary's church contains a display of medieval craftsmanship and elsewhere there's ancient woodland and a former tannery. Part of the walk passes through the hamlet of Moats Tye and afterwards Little London. During the summer months you can watch leather against willow at the local cricket field, and maybe rub shoulders with local celebrity, and former TV cook, Delia Smith who lives nearby.

The Gardeners Arms

This small pub is thought to have originated around the middle of the 19th century, being described as a beerhouse in Upper Combs. Nowadays the friendly pub is run on traditional lines where patrons can relax without the distraction of fruit machines and jukebox. Wholesome pub grub such as ham, egg and chips, sausage and mash, cottage pie, along with a variety of sandwiches, can be eaten in the dining room and bar area. Picnic tables are available outside where you can watch local cricket matches. The Gardeners Arms is a freehouse and contains a selection of Greene King and Adnams beers. From time to time new beers brewed locally are introduced. Telephone: 01449 673963.

THE WALK

Leave the car park and turn left to join a quiet surfaced lane. Continue ahead, ignoring a left fork at the next junction, through **Moats Tye** and **Little London**. Carry on straight ahead to shortly pass **Bluehouse Farm** buildings and reach a spot on the map marked **Halfpenny Hall**.

Why the oddly named Halfpenny Hall (nowadays a small thatched cottage) and Pennyplot House just around the corner? Maybe the titles were part of some monetary transaction associated with the properties when they were originally built. The names have long puzzled locals and no one has yet come up with a plausible answer.

Swing left through a hedge gap in front near a fingerpost and continue on a field edge path with a hedge on the left. Pass **Holyoak Farm** and maintain direction along a broad grassy path to reach the edge of **Combs Wood**. Go forward a few paces to reach a fingerpost and entrance to the wood.

You may wish to make a short detour here into the wood which is mentioned in the Domesday Book. *The best time to visit is during the months of April and May when bird song and wild flowers are at their best. The ancient art of coppicing - letting in light to encourage further growth - is a regular feature here with harvested timber made available for local firewood.*

Turn left onto a cross field path and climb three successive stiles to enter **St Mary's churchyard**.

To explore the church, a key may be obtained from the rectory, telephone 01449 612076. Inside the spacious building you'll find some lovely carved bench ends, some in the likeness of people and others in the likeness of animals.

Gradually make your way round to the front of the church and follow a gravel access path, which soon becomes surfaced, to arrive at **Church Road**. Turn right here, continue along the road for about 200 yards and then turn left to join a field edge path with a watercourse on the right. Maintain direction and later turn right over a footbridge.

Drive and Stroll

Head up a grassy path to arrive at **Tannery Road**.

Cross the road and turn left to continue on a footway. Pass Webb's Close and look left to see the site and some former buildings belonging to **Combs Tannery**.

In its heyday the tannery, established in 1711, employed many of the village population. To prepare the leather, raw cattle hides were dipped into a pit filled with ground oak bark, a smelly but necessary task. Afterwards the tanned hides were scrubbed and polished before being manufactured into finished products such as leather belts and fire buckets. The tannery finally ceased production in 1988, a victim of changing times and economic circumstances.

The Gardeners Arms at Combs

Turn right by a fingerpost just past a factory entrance to join a field edge path. Keep forward with attractive parkland on the right to eventually turn left into **Mill Lane**. Continue up the hill, passing **Westend Farm** and the **Old Mill House** as you go. Just as you draw level with **Oak View Cottage**, turn left through a hedge gap to enter a cultivated field. The path runs gently downhill to the bottom of a shallow valley, passing a lone dead tree on the way. Enter the next field and climb up the other side where the path swings right and left to meet the **Stowmarket** to **Battisford** road at the top. Turn right here and the **Gardeners Arms** is just ahead on the left.

PLACES OF INTEREST NEARBY

Just south of Stowmarket at Cotton is the **Mechanical Music Museum and Bygones**. It contains an extensive collection of fairground organs, as well as smaller musical boxes and street pianos. Demonstrations include music played on a mighty Wurlitzer theatre organ. Telephone: 01449 613876.

12 | Needham Market

The wooden sculpture beside the lake at Needham Market

The Walk 2 miles ⏱1½ hours
Map Explorer 211 Bury St Edmunds & Stowmarket (GR 094547)

How to get there

Leave the A14 Bury St Edmunds to Ipswich road at the A140 Beacon Hill interchange and follow the B1078 to Needham Market. Buses (High Street) and trains (BR Station) stop about 10 minutes' walk from the start. **Parking**: Pay and display car park at Needham Lake.

Drive and Stroll

Introduction

This easy walk might be described as out by the riverside and home by the lake. Ideal for families with youngsters, the walk starts from Needham Lake, a popular focal point in the largely rural Gipping Valley. Tables are available here for picnics with a children's play area nearby. A hard surface, suitable for wheelchair users, encircles the lake. A small visitors' centre, with toilets, gives information on what to see and do. The walk partially follows the Gipping Valley towpath in the direction of Stowmarket, with the option of returning via Needham High Street.

Alder Carr Farm

The farm shop (open Tuesday to Sunday and Bank Holiday Mondays) sells locally grown produce along with pick-your-own fruits during the season. A traditional tearoom serves teas, coffee, snacks and light lunches. Be sure to taste the ice cream, made locally in fourteen different flavours – absolutely delicious. If you need something more substantial, there are food outlets in and around Needham High Street. Other attractions at the farm include a small recreational area for children and a number of craft shops. A farmers' market is held on the third Saturday of each month. Telephone: 01449 720820.

THE WALK

With the lake on the left, go past a wooden sculpture and cross an arched bridge in front. Turn sharp left onto the **Gipping Valley Footpath**, take the tarmac path and continue ahead with the lake over to the left. Ignore a path forking right that takes you to a small wild wood area.

Hereabouts, there's usually a small noticeboard listing up-to-date details of birds that have been caught and released within the local area.

Continue beside the river, passing as you go some pretty houses and gardens that almost back onto the river.

It's difficult to imagine nowadays but this narrow stretch of river once had horse-drawn barges passing by, plying their trade on a 17-mile route between Ipswich and Stowmarket. Some 200 navvies with their picks and shovels built

15 locks to turn the river into a navigable canal. Open for traffic in 1793, cargoes that were carried upstream included timber, stone, coal and slates, with malt and grain going in the opposite direction. As a result, inland trade, which hitherto suffered from badly-maintained turnpike roads, was given a huge boost; the cost of transportation is said to have been reduced by a half. With the coming of the railway, by 1900 waterborne trade had almost ceased and the navigation finally closed in 1934.

Bear right through a kissing gate to proceed along a narrow surfaced path. Shortly bear left across some grass and head towards a road bridge in front. Pass under the bridge, still on the towpath. A nearby water sluice enables the normally slow-moving river to speed up.

As you head your way upstream towards Stowmarket, the Gipping now resembles something like a mini 19th-century industrial highway, although it was probably

Drive and Stroll

much wider and deeper at the time. Soon it progresses through a pastoral scene of lowland meadows and open countryside. However, in late summer the river surface is often covered in stretches of algae and choked with reeds and rushes.

The tower of St Mary's church at Creeting St Mary can be seen away to the right. Other paths take you up to the church where there are attractive views over the Gipping valley.

 ④

At **Raven's Farm** turn left over a bridge with metal railings and head up a path with a railway crossing at the far end. Before reaching the crossing, turn left through a kissing gate and continue on a broad grassy path with a tree plantation on the right. Later pass some stables and arrive at a T-junction. Turn right here into **Hawks Mill Street** if you wish to return by the High Street. Otherwise turn left to walk back to the lake.

The large brick building of Hawks Mill in front, now converted into flats, was built in 1884. A mill was recorded here in the Domesday Book. *In later centuries it became a fulling mill, connected perhaps with local cloth manufacture.*

 ⑤

Go past the mill, continue to the bridge ahead and bear right down some steps. If you wish to visit **Alder Carr Farm**, follow the driveway as signposted. Otherwise, carry on along the surfaced path previously walked, pass through a kissing gate and swing right and left over a bridge to enter **Crown Street**. Maintain direction to enter a grassy area known locally as the Camping Land. Stay on the left edge to reach **King's Field Nature Reserve**.

According to a local information leaflet, the meadow was once used by knights for jousting practice. Nowadays you'll find a quiet area planted with native trees and plants. Over to the right across station field is the railway station opened in 1846. Nowadays, intercity express trains running between Norwich and London thunder through here every day.

 ⑥

When you eventually arrive at a gate on the left, fork right a few paces to reach a surfaced path that encircles the lake. Turn left or right, either will return you back to your start point.

The imposing Hawks Mill is now flats

PLACES OF INTEREST NEARBY

Stonham Barns Leisure Complex is home to the Suffolk Owl Sanctuary and there are birds of prey from Britain and around the world, some of which feature in flying displays. The 90-acre site also contains craft and specialist workshops, a garden centre and golf course. Located on the Al 120 at Stonham Aspal. Tel: 01449 711755.

13 | Nayland

The river Stour running through Nayland

The Walk 4 miles ⏱ 2½ hours
Map OS Explorer 196 Sudbury, Hadleigh & Dedham Vale (GR 973340)

How to get there

From Colchester take the A134 towards Sudbury. After Great Horkesley take the first right turning into Nayland. From Ipswich take the A12 south and turn onto the B1068 to Higham, Stoke-by-Nayland and thence to Nayland. **Parking**: Road lay-by standing beside the Horkesley Road on the southern side of Nayland village.

Introduction

This absorbing walk takes place on the edge of Constable country in an area designated as one of outstanding natural beauty. Historically the small picturesque village of Nayland, (not to be confused with nearby Stoke-by-Nayland), is another former cloth centre nestling in the Stour Valley. Its fortunes fluctuated from wealth in the later Middle Ages to gradual stagnation in succeeding centuries. There are a number of period properties to admire, including streets, cottages and houses of the Tudor and Stuart period.

After leaving Nayland, the walk gains some height, affording fine views of the local landscape. You won't come across too many ploughed fields. Much of the route includes stretches of pasture, where sheep and cattle can often be seen grazing. A highlight of the walk is undoubtedly towards the finish,

Drive and Stroll

where the impressive sight of landscaped rear gardens running down to the riverside catches the eye.

The Anchor

The Anchor enjoys a tranquil location situated next to the Stour. You can eat your meal outside on the terrace beside a bank that slopes down to the riverside. Walls inside the bar area are adorned with pictures and prints of characters and events relating to a bygone age. The pub prides itself on providing good food sourced from local produce. A comprehensive menu includes tasty bar snacks such as soups, stews, pies and a delicious assortment of sandwiches. In the stylish restaurant smoked fish and meat dishes are available. For drinks you'll find Greene King, Adnams and other guest ales. The Anchor was one of the earliest pubs in the county to declare a non-smoking policy. Telephone: 01206 262313.

THE WALK

From the lay-by head towards **Nayland** village, passing the river and **Anchor pub** as you go. Enter **Court Street** and then the narrow **High Street**.

Take a look at some of the buildings, including the local post office where the sorting boxes and modes of mail delivery can be seen through the window. Over the way is a milestone obelisk, looking for all the world like a market cross.

St James' church across the street is well worth a visit, both inside and outside. The altar piece is one of Constable's sacred paintings, 'Christ Blessing the Bread and Wine,' which he painted in 1809. A one-time vicar here, Revd William Jones (1777-1800)

composed the well-known hymn tune St Stephen which is still in use today.

Further ahead stands the White Hart, an old coaching inn, whose front tunnel entrance was big enough for a carriage to pass through.

Pass over the bridge at **Mill Street**, bear right at the next road junction and continue ahead. At the next road entrance turn left and proceed up **Gravel Hill**. Most of the road walking on the route - about half a mile - is along this stretch of minor road. Ignore a path going left and carry on to where the road bends right. Here, turn left by a fingerpost to join the descending old earth lane known as **Farthings Lane**. At the bottom cross a stile and enter a field, continuing along the left edge.

Through hedge gaps you catch a glimpse of the tall tower of St Mary's church standing on a hill top at Stoke-by-Nayland. Walking now is mostly through fields of pasture amongst idyllic and peaceful countryside.

 ③

Go through a kissing gate into the adjoining field. Where the hedge ends, veer right via another kissing gate into more pasture. Carry on over the crest of a hill and down the other side to cross a stile at the bottom. Go down some steps and turn left to join a green earth lane.

On the right edge is Stoke-by-Nayland golf course. Through the hedgerows there are delightful views of the landscaped course beyond a fringe of trees.

 ④

Maintain direction, pass the entrance to **Beacham's Farm**, to later arrive at **Thompsons Farm**, a substantial farm house on the right. Go forward a few paces and turn left onto an access path leading to **Spring Farm**. Shortly before reaching the farm, turn right onto a diverted path and pass a large barn on the left. Follow the downhill path and soon bear left by a large pond. Turn left through a gap and continue down a lovely grassy path hemmed in by leafy hedgerows either side. Cross a stile at the bottom and afterwards head up and down the right field edge. A kissing

Gravel Hill, Nayland

gate gives access to woodland, composed mostly of bracken and trees.

 ⑤

Leave the wood and continue ahead to an arable field. Veer left across the field, aiming for a hedge gap the other side. Cross a track, maintain direction and continue with trees on the right. Go past **Townland Barn** where the path shortly narrows with sapling trees and a hedgerow either side, soon to emerge into open countryside.

Pause for a while here to admire the stunning spectacle of the Stour valley set out in front. From the high ground there are superb views

Drive and Stroll

across the border into Essex and beyond.

Take the descending path through pasture to enter woodland at **Harper's Grove**. Briefly pass through more woodland and afterwards cross a sleeper bridge and three stiles in fairly quick succession. In a smaller meadow, look in the left corner for a stile which brings you onto a narrow path. Pass a brick boundary wall and school playing field to eventually reach **Bear Street**. Cross the latter, turn right and continue along a footway. Just before reaching a bus shelter, bear left onto short stretch of tarmac and afterwards cross a large green sward. Immediately after crossing a river bridge, turn sharp left down an embankment to walk beside the water.

Attractive houses with their rear gardens running down to the river quickly catch the eye, especially during the springtime when the green foliage is at its best.

Keep following the path to eventually climb some steps and out onto road. Turn right for the departure lay-by and left for Anchor.

PLACES OF INTEREST NEARBY

Colchester Castle, 6 miles due south of Nayland, was once known as Camulodunum and was the capital of Roman Britain. The castle was built after the Norman conquest on the foundations of the Roman Temple of Claudius. Period artefacts and displays are included in a fascinating interactive feature of see, hear, touch and discover. Tel: 01206 282939.

14 Flatford and Dedham

The bridge over the river Stour at Flatford

The Walk 2½ miles 🕐 1½ hours – longer if visiting Dedham
Map OS Explorer 196 Sudbury, Hadleigh & Dedham Vale (GR 075333)

How to get there

From the Ipswich or Colchester direction, take the A12 and approximately 7 miles south-east of Ipswich turn off at East Bergholt to join the B1070. Follow the latter through East Bergholt village and look for a signposted road (one-way system) direct to the hamlet of Flatford – about half a mile further on. **Parking**: Large landscaped car park privately owned and located at the top of Flatford Lane. Parking fee payable at the entrance.

Drive and Stroll

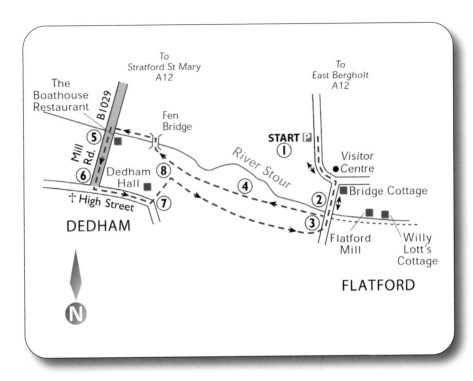

Introduction

If possible, choose a bright clear day to fully appreciate the verdant colours and hues of countryside contained in this area of outstanding natural beauty. The walk to Dedham Vale and back passes through a local landscape immortalised by the famous landscape artist, John Constable. If you are an admirer of his paintings, there's the extra bonus of visiting locations captured by Constable in paintings including *Hay Wain*, *Flatford Mill* and *River Stour*. Other Constable connections include an exhibition on his art, his old grammar school and Dedham church. Walking by the banks of the Stour, you may encounter artists sketching and painting the countryside just as Constable did.

Bridge House Tea Room

This excellent tea room is run by the National Trust. Light lunches consisting of soup, jacket potatoes with different fillings and pies are served. Scones and sandwiches along with tea, coffee and soft drinks are also available. Telephone: 01206 298260.

THE WALK

Exit the car park by an information display board in the bottom left corner and take a descending path to reach the road. Turn right and proceed down the road.

With the National Trust's Bridge Cottage in front, turn left here if you want to visit Willy Lott's cottage, remaining much as it was in Constable's Hay Wain.

Cross the bridge over the river Stour.

Turn left to visit the front of **Flatford Mill** *once owned by Constable's wealthy merchant father, Golding.*

Pass through two kissing gates onto the flood plain meadows. Walk beside the meandering river, its banks containing the gnarled trunks of willow trees that lean over and almost touch the ground. Continue through the lush pasture in front, often grazed by herds of cattle. Alongside on the river, rowing boats have replaced the heavy grain barges that once glided by. Straight ahead is the impressive tower of **Dedham church** which can be visited later.

Proceed through a large gap and over a shallow water channel and afterwards veer right towards the arched **Fen Bridge**. Cross the latter and turn left to join a narrow path taking you to **Dedham**. Cross three metal stiles in fairly quick succession, later a wooden one, and stay by the river to eventually reach the B1029 ahead. Go up some steps, through a kissing gate and turn left into **Mill Road**.

Just after passing the county border into Essex is the Boathouse Restaurant, another place where you can obtain food and drink.

Carry on to the road junction in front and enter **Dedham High Street** where you'll find more pubs and tearooms.

Turn left and continue along the busy high street.

Just across the road is the old grammar school. Now Grade I listed, this wonderful building was where a young John Constable came to school but learnt not a lot according to his headmaster.

Pass the Arts and Crafts building on the right. Proceed to where the road

Drive and Stroll

Flatford Mill

 (8)

soon curves right, cross a driveway and turn left to join a gravel track. Leave the track where it bends left towards **Dedham Hall** and veer fractionally right. Follow the path to a National Trust sign (**Dedham Hall Farm**) and pass through a metal kissing gate. Here the overhanging hedgerow provides a lovely tunnel effect.

Pass through more meadowland, go under power lines and veer slightly right towards a kissing gate near the hedge. Turn right through two kissing gates and continue ahead. **Fen Bridge** will appear once again away to the left. Carry straight on over the flood plain and make your way back to **Flatford** and the car park.

PLACES OF INTEREST NEARBY

Castle House in Dedham was the home of the late Sir Alfred Munnings, a past president of the Royal Academy. He is famous for his paintings of the rural landscape and studies of race horses. Telephone: 01206 322127.

5 | Kersey

The 14th-century Bell Inn, Kersey

The Walk 2½ miles ⏲ 1½ hours
Map OS Explorer No 196 Sudbury, Hadleigh & Dedham Vale
(GR 000443)

How to get there

Kersey village lies 10 miles west of Ipswich and 2½ miles from Hadleigh. From Ipswich take the A1071 to Hadleigh and then follow the A1141. From Stowmarket take the B1115 through Bildeston and later join the A1141. From either direction turn off at Kersey Mill and take a minor road signposted to Kersey (about 2 miles). **Parking**: Park in the main street with due care and consideration for others.

Drive and Stroll

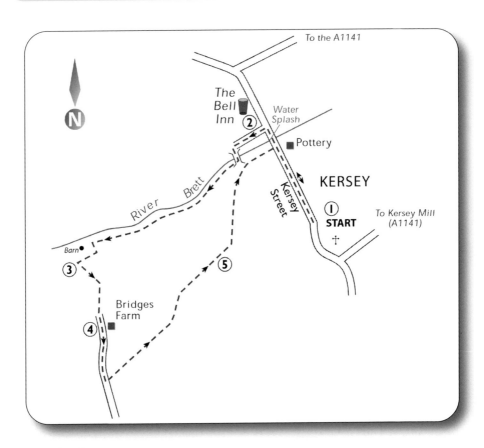

Introduction

The small picture-postcard village of Kersey is unusual in that it was built across the valley rather than along it. During the Middle Ages, when weaving was a cottage industry, local weavers produced a coarse-ribbed cloth, which became known as Kersey cloth. There's even a mention of it in one of Shakespeare's plays: 'Henceforth my wooing mind shall be expressed in russet yeas and honest kersey noes.' (*Love's Labour's Lost*, Act 5, Scene 2).

Kersey never quite gained prominence in terms of status and wealth, unlike the neighbouring wool towns such as Lavenham and Long Melford, whose legacy can be found in their magnificent churches. However, Kersey church should not be overlooked. Climb the steps to reach St Mary's, which stands aloof on a hill at one end of the main street, and you will be rewarded with stupendous views over the village and beyond. The church is noted for its fine porch, one of the best of its kind in the county.

The Bell Inn

The half-timbered Bell Inn, dating from the 14th century, nestles comfortably beside period cottages halfway up the village street. Inside you'll find oak beams and a flagstone floor. For a light bite try the flat bread filled with a selection of delicious fillings. From the changing main menu board you can choose from dishes such as ham, egg and chips, lasagne and cottage pie. For desserts there's a choice of home-made puddings and ice cream sundae. Ales include Adnams and Greene King, plus a weekly guest beer. This is a popular pub and booking is advised, especially at weekends. There's a car park for patrons and beer garden at the rear. Telephone: 01473 823229

THE WALK

①

From the church end of the village, make your way towards one of the most photographed scenes in Suffolk, the famous water splash – in reality the **river Brett** flowing unhampered through the village.

Take time to explore the various openings leading from the street, each with its mixture of tiles and over-hanging thatched cottages, a popular location for artists capturing the idyllic scene. The old village water pump encased in wood stands at the top of the hill.

②

Just before reaching the **Bell Inn**, turn left by a property named **Kedges End**. Continue along a short stretch of surfaced lane and then a grassy path. Ignore a path going right by some garden allotments and shortly bear left to continue on a narrower path. Go over a footbridge, up some steps in the bank and turn right. Keep following the stream, often choked in places by dense vegetation, until you eventually meet a squeezer stile. Swing left and right here to enter some pasture. Cross two stiles in quick succession to enter more pasture.

③

Head towards the left of a dilapidated barn ahead and into the field corner. Turn left through a metal gate to follow a farm access track, which soon curves right and heads up a field edge to reach **Bridges Farm**. Walk through the farmyard.

Look right for a barn door and if it is open, stand on the path and take a peep inside. On the far wall is a colourful display of rosettes won by the farmer's pedigree sheep and cattle at shows over a 20-year period.

Drive and Stroll

Shortly join a surfaced lane with high hedgerows either side. After about another 300 yards leave the lane and turn left onto a cross field path, which shortly passes under some power lines. Pass an enclosed pond on the left and carry on by a broad grassy path to the boundary. Bear right and left here to find a rising field edge path with a hedge on the left.

The tall tower of Kersey church standing majestically on high ground at one end of the village will shortly appear in front. Stretches of undulating countryside combined with the colours and variety of arable crops, mature hedgerows and a wealth of trees, along with Kersey village itself nestling in a valley – all add up to offer one of the most scenic views in Suffolk.

Keep following the path to reach a stile situated by an electricity pole.

Should you encounter a notice indicating 'Bull In Field', carry straight on and turn left at the road ahead. Otherwise, cross the stile and walk parallel with the power lines on a descending path, passing an enclosed water reservoir as you go. Cross a stile and carry on to the boundary to turn right over another stile. Stay on part of the path previously walked but ignore a path going left over a bridge. Cross another stile and shortly pass the house where the famous author of adventure novels, Ralph Hammond Innes, once lived. Carry on ahead to reach the main street and return to your point of departure.

Occupying the site of some old stables across the road is Kersey Pottery. Established in 1982, the small studio produces a wide selection of stoneware and porcelain.

PLACES OF INTEREST NEARBY

Corn Craft, in nearby Monks Eleigh, is a unique business based on the traditional craft of making corn dollies. Craftsmen and women make the hundred or so designs from locally-grown natural wheat. There's a craft and gift shop on site, along with a tearoom. Telephone: 01449 740456.

16 Lavenham

The church of St Peter and St Paul, Lavenham

The Walk 1¼ miles 🕐 1 hour
Map OS Explorer No 196 Sudbury, Hadleigh & Dedham Vale (GR 913496)

How to get there

Lavenham is situated on the A1141 about 10 miles south of Bury St Edmunds. It is also signposted from the B1115. **Parking**: Free car parking (at present) is available on the public car park opposite the church.

Drive and Stroll

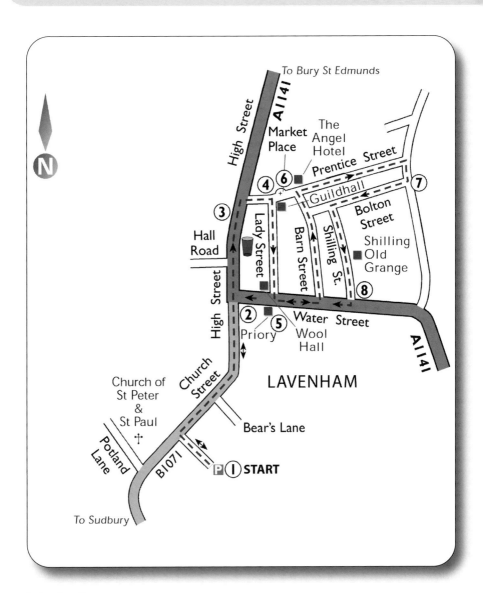

Introduction

Walk around Lavenham's medieval grid system of narrow streets and alleyways and you'll be following in the footsteps of Flemish weavers and rich clothiers who made the village wealthy from the proceeds of the Suffolk wool trade. Indeed, 16th-century Lavenham became so prosperous, at one time it was reckoned to be the fourteenth wealthiest town in England. A century later, however, trade began to decline with merchants and weavers moving elsewhere. Fortuitously, in the absence of a major fire and the arrival of new industry, Lavenham had been left with a legacy of timber framed houses and cottages that were never replaced or updated. If the old weavers returned they would recognise the scene straight away – minus their looms, of course!

Although this is a short stroll, it should not be rushed. Slowly does it as you soak up the medieval atmosphere, mingling amongst some of Lavenham's 350 listed properties. At least you won't need to wear stout footwear - all of the walking is done on a metalled surface.

The Greyhound

This family-run pub dating from the 14th century lies snug amongst listed buildings in the High Street. From the pub's front windows you look out straight across the street to the Crooked House. The Greyhound offers both light and hot meals. There's a large selection of sandwiches - plain or toasted, soup, ploughman's, jacket potatoes with different fillings and delicious omelettes. Main dishes include fish, steaks, lasagne and surprisingly a selection of Austrian cuisine. Drinks include Greene King Abbot and IPA, plus other guest ales. Outside there's a beer garden and patio area. Children are welcome here. Telephone: 01787 247475

If it's a tearoom you're after, you won't be disappointed. There is one placed every few hundred yards or so along the High Street and elsewhere.

THE WALK

①

From the car park turn right to join **Church Street**.

Walk down the street and immediately be confronted with some glorious half-timbered houses. Little wonder that Lavenham is often described as the finest preserved medieval town in England. Even power and telephone cables have been buried

underground to preserve the town's character.

②

Pass **Water Street** at the bottom of the hill, a clue to a much-needed resource in cloth manufacture, and make your way up the **High Street**, passing the **Swan Hotel** as you go. Look left for the appropriately named **Crooked House** (now an art gallery) leaning at an impossible angle opposite the **Greyhound pub**.

Carrying on further along the High

Drive and Stroll

Street reveals nothing of note unless you wish to visit the post office or look for more tearooms. The start of the 3-mile circular Lavenham railway walk is a little further on.

Turn right into **Market Lane** where a narrow thoroughfare brings you onto the **Market Place**, the heart of Lavenham's past.

Over to the right is the Guildhall built in 1528-29 for the Corpus Christi Guild. On the corner is a carved figure said to be that of John de Vere, 15th Earl of Oxford and founder of the guild. In later years the building has served as a prison, almshouse and wool store.

Turn right to join **Lady Street** and shortly pass the local Tourist Information Office. Just before the road junction ahead note the **Old Wool Hall** on the right, now part of the **Swan Hotel**.

Turn left into **Water Street** with the **Priory** opposite. Turn left again and proceed up **Barn Street**, back towards the **Market Place**.

The orange-ochre and colour-washed building on the right is the 14th-century Little Hall, nowadays home of the Suffolk Preservation Society. On the left is the Market Cross dating back to 1502.

Turn right and pass between the 15th-century **Angel Hotel** and the **Great House Restaurant** to join **Prentice Street**. Pass the small car park and toilets on the left.

In front are views of an undulating landscape, comprising mainly arable fields full of sticky clay soil.

Turn right at the bottom and go right again to walk up **Bolton Street**. Take the turning on the left, **Shilling Street**, to pass **Shilling Old Grange**.

According to popular legend, it was here that schoolgirl Jane Taylor, daughter of a local engraver, wrote the popular nursery rhyme 'Twinkle, Twinkle Little Star'.

At the road boundary turn right into **Water Street** and then left to rejoin **Church Street** and back towards the car park.

No walk around Lavenham would be complete without a visit to the grand church of St Peter and St Paul, a short distance away from the finish. It is noticeable for its 140 ft tower and dominates the local countryside. It was generous clothiers, grown wealthy in the wool trade, who provided finance for church building, the legacy of which can be seen today.

17 | Long Melford

The village green at Long Melford

The Walk 3½ miles ⏱2 hours
Map OS Explorer 196 Sudbury, Hadleigh & Dedham Vale (GR 865466)

How to get there

Long Melford village is some 12 miles south of Bury St Edmunds and 3 miles north of Sudbury. From Bury take the A134 and leave it to join the A1092 just before entering Long Melford. The large village green is on the right. From Sudbury take the A134 and join the B1064 at a roundabout. Stay on the B1064, pass through the two-mile village High Street and shortly turn left to briefly join the A1092. After about 200 yards quickly turn right for parking. **Parking**: Beside Church Road or on the large village green.

Drive and Stroll

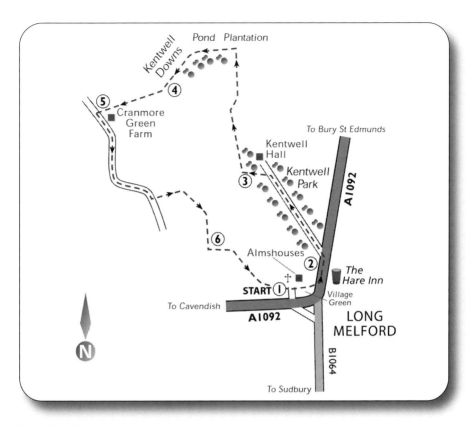

Introduction

Nowadays, with a plethora of shops selling antiques plus its association with the TV series *Lovejoy*, much of which was filmed locally, Long Melford is often known as the antiques capital of East Anglia. This interesting walk, however, steers away from the hustle and bustle of the main street and explores some of the relative quietness found in the surrounding landscape. Attractions include Melford's large green, flanked on the north side by Holy Trinity, a church of cathedral-like proportions and a must for those who like to explore historic churches. Later on, the walk passes Kentwell Hall, a magnificent moated Tudor building open to the public and noted for its themed events. An area marked on the map as Kentwell Downs provides a pleasant interlude. From here the path gently descends to reach Cranmore Green Farm. The return route takes you along tracks beside mature hedgerows and afterwards enters lush pasture in Church Fields and back to the green.

The Hare Inn

Standing beside the A1092 and almost opposite the driveway to Kentwell Hall, is the Hare Inn. A comprehensive menu is offered – everything from light snacks to substantial meals. Roast lamb, sausage egg and chips, scampi and lasagne are among the popular dishes. Baguettes, sandwiches, burgers and soup feature among the lighter fare. There is also a wide range of dessert dishes from which to choose. You can eat in the bar or in the restaurant, and there is also a large beer garden to relax in. Telephone: 01787 310379.

THE WALK

Start the walk by crossing the large green in front of some benches positioned in front of a brick wall belonging to **Trinity Hospital** (Tudor almshouses). Continue over the green to the corner where a public toilet building is hidden beyond a hedge on the left. Turn left onto a walkway running beside the A1092 and shortly bear left to join the ¼ mile long driveway leading up to **Kentwell Hall**.

Veer left to join a grassy path that runs parallel to the driveway.

Note the pollarded lime trees situated either side and look left over your shoulder for more stunning views of Holy Trinity church as you go.

Just before reaching the main entrance at **Kentwell Hall**, the path heads left into a small area of trees. Pass through two gates in quick succession and leave the track to take a grassy path with a hedge on the left. Exit by a springer stile to rejoin the track. Carry on ahead for another 400 yards and turn left by a fingerpost to skirt **Pond Plantation**. Continue on the slowly descending field edge path along **Kentwell Downs**, also part of **Stour Valley Path**.

At a marker post bear right onto a cross-field path through an arable field.

The church seen on a hill away to the right amongst rolling countryside is that of Glemsford.

Cross a footbridge into a grassy area and shortly pass between some buildings at **Cranmore Green Farm** to eventually reach the road ahead. Turn left to join the B1066 and after about 350 yards leave the road and turn left onto a rising

The moated Kentwell Hall dates from

concreted field entrance. The path later develops into a farm access track.

 ⑥

Stay on the track where it swings right and bear right at the next corner to join a cross-field path. Shortly ignore a path going right and continue ahead with a hedge on the right. Cross a footbridge over a ditch, with the hedge now on the left. Follow the hedgeline round to reach the bottom corner. Just before reaching a large oak tree, turn left into **Church Fields** and head towards a paddock with a rail fence. Stay beside the fence and head up towards the church as waymarked. Pass the church on left and return to the point of departure.

PLACES OF INTEREST NEARBY

Melford Hall is a turreted red-brick Tudor house, set in spacious surroundings which were originally a medieval hunting park. Home of the Hyde Parker family since 1786, it is now owned by the National Trust. Telephone: 01787 880286.

18 Bury St Edmunds

The award-winning Abbey Gardens with the church of St James beyond

The Walk 3 miles ⏱2 hours
Map OS Explorer 211 Bury St Edmunds & Stowmarket (GR 866624). A street map covering this walk might be useful, and can be obtained from the Tourist Information office on Angel Hill, 2 minutes walk from the Abbey Gardens.

How to get there

Nowton Country Park can be found 2 miles south of Bury St Edmunds town centre. Take the A14 Ipswich to Bury St Edmunds road then go south on the signposted A134. Pass some flower and seed nurseries on the left and proceed to the second of two roundabouts where you take the road signposted to Nowton Country Park. The park entrance is about half a mile further on. **Parking**: Plenty of space within the designated parking area.

Drive and Stroll

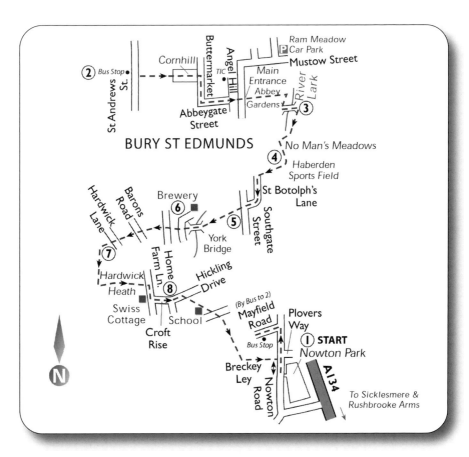

Introduction

This walk, featuring a vista of Bury St Edmunds is full of historical interest and is the only linear route in the book. The walk takes you via the ruins of a once great Benedictine abbey, through stunning floral gardens, along the town's backwaters and over Hardwick Heath, noted for its fine specimen trees. After parking in Nowton Country Park you can catch a bus (Telephone: 01284 702020 for current timetable details) into Bury St Edmunds town centre and start the walk there. Alternatively you can park on the Angel Hill or Ram Meadow (about 5 minutes walk from the Abbey Gardens) and bus back, or retrace the route taken at the beginning of the walk.

Nowton Country Park (Telephone: 01284 763666) contains some 200 acres of beautiful Suffolk countryside, landscaped over 100 years ago in typical Victorian style. There is a children's play area and light refreshments are obtainable from a kiosk. The 55-acre Hardwick Heath contains fine specimen trees, some of which have plaques giving details of their history.

Rushbrooke Arms

There is a fair selection of cafés and pubs in Bury St Edmunds but I have chosen one situated in Sicklesmere, a village less than a mile away from Nowton Park beside the A134. The pub with a thatched roof offers traditional pub grub, some of it home-made, with generous portions. On Sundays there's a special carvery. For drinks, Greene King real ales are on offer, with a selection of draught beers including Fosters, Carling, Guinness, Strongbow Cider and wines. Tea and coffee is also served which you can enjoy in the beer garden if the weather is fine. Telephone: 01284 388242.

THE WALK

Walk past the main entrance to the park and shortly turn left by a noticeboard. Continue to the road and turn right onto a footway. Pass **Plovers Way** and later turn left into **Mayfield Road** (about 200 yards). The bus shelter is left of the small roundabout.

Alight at the bus stop in **St Andrews Street North** at the back of Woolworths. Cross the road and go down a narrow alleyway that leads onto the **Cornhill Market Place**. Cross the latter straight ahead and turn right at the far end. Go along the **Buttermarket** and then left into pedestrianised **Abbeygate Street** to reach **Angel Hill**. Go forward to enter the **Abbey Gardens** through the main surviving gateway.

Walking down the main avenue you'll find the scattered remains of a once powerful and wealthy Benedictine abbey. Following his death at the hand of the invading Danes, the remains of the martyred Saxon King Edmund were brought here which led to the building of the abbey. Thus the great abbey of St Edmundsbury began in 1063 and later became a popular place of pilgrimage. Its grandeur remained until the dissolution of the monasteries in 1539 when its wealth was transferred to the Crown. Decline gradually set in and nowadays only the ruins serve as a reminder of the abbey's former glory.

The international prize-winning Abbey Gardens draw visitors from near and far, especially during the summer months. Look right and you'll see the cathedral church of St James, with its magnificent Gothic lantern tower completed in 2005, after five years of construction.

Drive and Stroll

The totem pole in Nowton Country Park

 ③

Continue ahead, pass a children's play area on the right and afterwards cross a bridge over the **river Lark**. Turn right onto a narrow surfaced path – the first of many. Maintain direction, go over a cycle way and shortly turn right to cross another river bridge. Just before meeting a second bridge, turn left into an area known as **No Man's Meadows**, a local nature reserve. Proceed through some low lying pasture and later pass under two sets of cables before crossing a bridge and going up steps to reach the **Haberden Sports Field**.

 ④

Turn right and follow the path to **St Botolph's Lane**. (Alternatively, in the interests of safety, stay inside the edge of the sports field which is what the locals appear to do.) Turn left and continue up the surfaced lane, taking care with the traffic coming towards you along a one-way system. At the junction with **Southgate Street** cross straight over. Turn left and quickly right onto a stony driveway with a stone boundary wall on the left.

 ⑤

Follow the driveway, which shortly becomes a narrow path, running between a hedge and wire fence. Shortly turn right to join a surfaced path that later takes you over **York Bridge**.

The area around here, containing many large mature trees, is liable to flooding. The aroma of yeast in the air comes from the Greene King brewery, located a short distance away.

Cross the brewery access road and take the next left turn, passing an old semi-circular kissing gate on the right. Cross **Cullum Road** in front, move slightly right and continue along another surfaced path. At a T-junction turn left and continue with a mature hedgerow either side. Head up the rising path in front and later cross **Barons Road**. Cross over **Hardwick Lane**, with the **West Suffolk** hospital on the right, and go on to **Hardwick Heath**.

Cross the heath and turn left by some fenced-off sports pitches. Turn

right at the boundary and, in a few paces, turn left, passing a block of changing rooms and public toilets, keeping them on the left.

Hardwick Heath contains a number of specimen trees, dominated by some mature Lebanese cedars. The heath has had a varied and interesting history, including use as a medieval grazing area by St Edmundsbury Abbey and being the site of a prisoner-of-war camp during the Second World War.

Go straight ahead over the heath and down a hill to locate and pass through a boundary gate. Afterwards, turn right and continue along **Home Farm Lane**.

On the right is a thatched cottage situated amongst a residential housing estate. Apparently the building used to be called Swiss Cottage and was once part of the local Cullum estate.

Turn left up **Croft Rise** and go left

PLACES OF INTEREST NEARBY

Moyses Hall Museum is an award-winning museum located in the market place of Bury St Edmunds. A diverse range of exhibits date from prehistoric times to the present. There are galleries devoted to the likes of hearth and home, the local gun trade, collections of the Suffolk Regiment and relics of the Red Barn Murder, including the death mask of murderer, William Corder. Tel: 01284 706185.

Drive and Stroll

again at the junction with **Hickling Drive**. Follow the latter to meet a stretch of woodland. Take a narrow path into the woodland and shortly emerge beside a panel fence to the rear of housing on the right. At the junction with **Hardwick Middle School** cross the road and turn left. With a meadow on the right, pass through a gap in the fence. Ignore a path going right and take the broad descending track down **Breckey Ley** to meet **Nowton Road** at the bottom. Turn right, continue along the footway and turn left through a space in the boundary wall back into **Nowton Park**.

19 | West Stow Country Park

The Anglo-Saxon village at West Stow (Image courtesy of St Edmundsbury Borough Council/West Stow Anglo-Saxon Village Trust)

The Walk 2½ miles ⏱ 1½ hours
Map OS Explorer 229 Thetford in The Brecks (GR 801715)

How to get there

From the A14 west of Bury St Edmunds take the B1106 and A1101 north, follow the brown tourist signs for 'Anglo-Saxon Village'. Just beyond the village of Lackford, turn right with the park entrance shortly appearing on the right. **Parking**: The official car park at West Stow Country Park.

Drive and Stroll

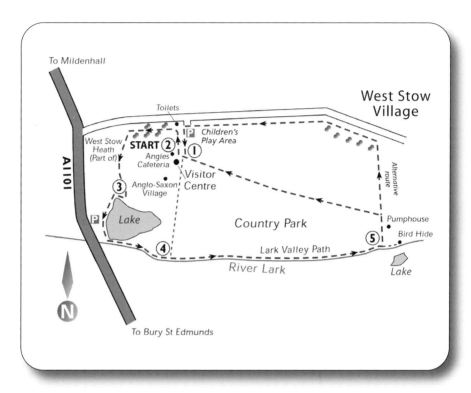

Introduction

This effortless walk – no stiles, no hills – takes you around the fringes of the 125-acre country park at West Stow. Along the way you'll find a reconstructed Anglo-Saxon village, a large lake, woodland glades, the Lark Valley Path, light soils and open heathland. The park was opened in 1979 and is managed by St Edmundsbury Borough Council. It is located on the southern edge of Breckland, a landscape of semi-wilderness characterised by heaths, forests and rows of Scots pine trees. The site, which annually attracts more than 100,000 visitors, is ideal for families with youngsters. There's a comprehensive play area and you can roam more or less at will within the park's boundaries.

Angles Cafeteria

Perched high above the ground, the cafeteria's balcony gives excellent views through the trees across the park. The balcony also overlooks a wild bird feeding area where various species can be seen obtaining food from hanging feeders. Up-to-date details of bird and wild animal sightings within the park are listed on a nearby board. Light refreshments on offer include a selection of coffee, tea, hot chocolate and soft drinks. There's also a choice of hot soups and sandwiches, sealed or panini style. Tel: 01284 728718. For a more substantial meal you could try the **Red Lion** in the neighbouring village of Icklingham. Tel: 01284 711698

THE WALK

From the car park make your way towards a fingerpost guiding you to the visitor centre and café.

From the visitor centre you can purchase a ticket to enter the site of an Anglo-Saxon Village (c. AD 420-650) which has been excavated and reconstructed using tools and techniques available at the time. Scattered around the site are primitive thatched huts, arable field crops, together with hens and a herd of pigs. There is also an exhibition of objects found on site and a display of the fashions of the era. From time to time, events are held where volunteers in period costume bring the village to life with demonstrations of Anglo-Saxon crafts such as woodwork, leatherwork, metalwork and cooking.

Otherwise or later, take the surfaced path and turn left just before reaching a toilet block ahead. The well-defined path, marked with a red arrow, runs parallel to the road

and takes you through a plantation of spruce and pine trees. Nearby display boards contain relevant background notes. The path eventually leads to the edge of **West Stow Heath**, a site of special scientific interest (SSSI). The way ahead is now marked by a blue arrow, which guides you through a series of gates before arriving at the edge of a lake.

The large lake, which attracts several species of wildfowl, was formerly a gravel pit, excavated to provide aggregate for the building of the nearby airfield at Lakenheath in the Second World War.

Turn right and walk round the perimeter of the lake, passing the fishermen's car park at the back. Keep following the lakeside and later pass between the lake and the **river Lark** running almost alongside. Maintain direction to join the **Lark Valley Path**.

The once navigable Lark runs for about 13 miles between Bury St Edmunds and Mildenhall. After it was canalized, around 1715, horse-drawn barges passed

Drive and Stroll

The old pump-house at West Stow

by, carrying shipments such as coal and malt. However, with the coming of the railway to Bury St Edmunds in 1884, river trade fell into a sharp decline and eventually led to the demise of local waterborne traffic.

 ④

Stay on the **Lark Valley Path** beside the river where it now runs straight ahead. If you wish to take a short-cut, follow the next path going left. Otherwise, in about another 200 yards, and near the visible remains of a river lock, swing left up a slight embankment and turn right at the top. (If you wish to visit a bird hide overlooking a lake at **Lackford**, carry straight on for about another 75 yards.)

 ⑤

Bear left at the boundary to arrive beside an old **pumphouse** building.

The old red-brick pumphouse was used up until the 1950s to pump sewage effluent into nearby lagoons, now covered and hidden.

Continue straight ahead along a partially surfaced road. After about 75 yards turn left through a gate and return to the start on grassland. If you wish to extend the walk (by about ½ mile or so), carrying on towards the far boundary in front and turn left. Whatever route you take, walk towards the visitor centre ahead and back to your point of departure.

20 | Kedington

A view of Kedington from our route

The Walk 3 miles ⏱2 hours
Map OS Explorer No 210 Newmarket & Haverhill (GR 705470)

How to get there

Kedington lies 2½ miles north-east of Haverhill. From Bury St Edmunds go south-west on the A143 Haverhill road and turn off as directed to Kedington. Take the first turning on the left entering the village and head towards the church. **Parking**: Lay-by opposite Kedington church. Please park with due care and consideration for others.

Drive and Stroll

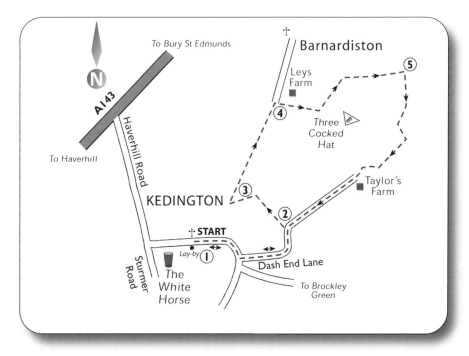

Introduction

Set in the far south-west corner of the county near the Essex border, Kedington, or Kitton as the locals call it, sits on a ridge overlooking the Stour valley. It's a quiet, thriving village set in an agricultural landscape. Standing apart from the village centre, is the church of St Peter and St Paul, open daily. Inside you'll find a treasure trove of history and really is a 'must see' on the walk. It positively encourages visitors and you may be lucky to have a personal tour escorted by a church member. The church, rich in monuments, is often referred to as the 'Westminster Abbey' of Suffolk and once inside it's not difficult to see why. The walk itself is highlighted by a series of lovely green lanes which, at one time, formed part of an ancient highway. You'll also find some pretty thatched cottages, with gardens to match.

The White Horse

Located in Sturmer Road, this is a popular village pub where you can expect a warm welcome and friendly atmosphere. The restaurant offers an excellent menu of home-cooked food. Main dishes include steaks and steak and ale pie, and a board proclaims home-made specials using local produce. For desserts there are things such as sticky toffee pudding, chocolate fudge and spotted dick. Real ales include Greene King IPA, Morlands and a guest beer. Families with well-behaved children are welcome. Outside is a large beer garden, ideal for sitting outside during warm weather. Telephone: 01440 763564.

THE WALK

Before or after the walk be sure to take a rewarding visit to the church on the opposite side of the road. After stooping low through the entrance door you'll encounter a haphazard arrangement of benches and pews standing on a brick floor. At the west end is the musician's gallery (c.1750). Attracting much attention is an early 17th-century three-decker pulpit. In the clerk's seat behind are hat pegs and nearby in the front nave pews is a wig-pole. An hourglass on a turned pole acted as a reminder to the preacher that his sermon time was nearly up. Elsewhere, there are monuments, beautifully sculpted, commemorating members of the Barnardiston family, who were the local lords of the manor.

Facing the church, turn right and walk along the footway for about 50 yards. Turn left, cross the road to join **Dash End Lane**. Follow this quiet lane, admiring the pretty thatched cottages and gardens in this neatly kept village as you go.

Leave the lane where it bears right and take **Taylor's Farm Road** going left. Just past the first bend turn left to join a field path, initially with a hedge on the left. Pass under power lines, cross the field and go over a small bridge at the far end to enter the adjoining field. According to the map, the path should run beside the right edge of the field. However, at the time of walking, the landowner seems to prefer walkers to cross the field, turn right and proceed diagonally to the top right-hand corner.

Join the first of a sequence of delightful green lanes with power lines running parallel to the left edge.

The rising lane, which has the appearance of a disused railway line save for its undulations, proceeds directly ahead. Amongst the wildflowers and grasses in the lane, botanists may discover the plant known as sulphur clover, usually found on clay soil. Seen in the summer months, its yellow flowers distinguish it from the common red and white clovers. The high ground gives spectacular views of cornfields, punctuated by wooded areas, for miles around. As you go downhill note the church of

Drive and Stroll

All Saints in Barnardiston, the village from which the Barnardiston family took their name. In the far distance appearing beyond some buildings you may just about spot Highpoint prison, standing in the village of Stradishall.

 ④

At the end of the lane, turn right to join a track that takes you past a boarded barn on the left and a red-brick house at **Leys Farm**. Follow the track round as it curves left to reach a broad grassy path lined with trees. Turn left by a marker post, proceed downhill and turn right at the bottom onto an ancient highway known as **Buntry Lane**.

This is another green lane with mature hedgerows that our ancestors used when moving from village to village, long before metalled roads appeared. Over to the right is a small private copse called the Three Cocked Hat, described as such because of its triangular shape.

 ⑤

Continue up the sloping lane to

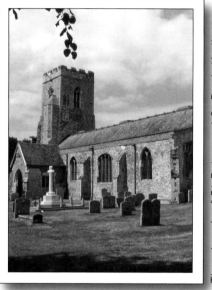

The church of St Peter and St Paul, Kedington

reach a lone elm tree. In another 50 yards ignore a path going left and stay on the lane as it swings right. Shortly the path runs downhill to eventually arrive at **Taylor's Farm**. Continue on the now surfaced lane to meet the point where you earlier joined a field edge path (Point 2). From here retrace your steps back to the church.

PLACES OF INTEREST NEARBY

The Ancient House Museum at nearby Clare is a 15th-century Grade I listed building and a fine example of the ancient art of pargeting – plaster on a wall with an ornamental pattern. Inside the museum there is a display of local history and photographs of bygone Clare. Telephone: 01787 277662.